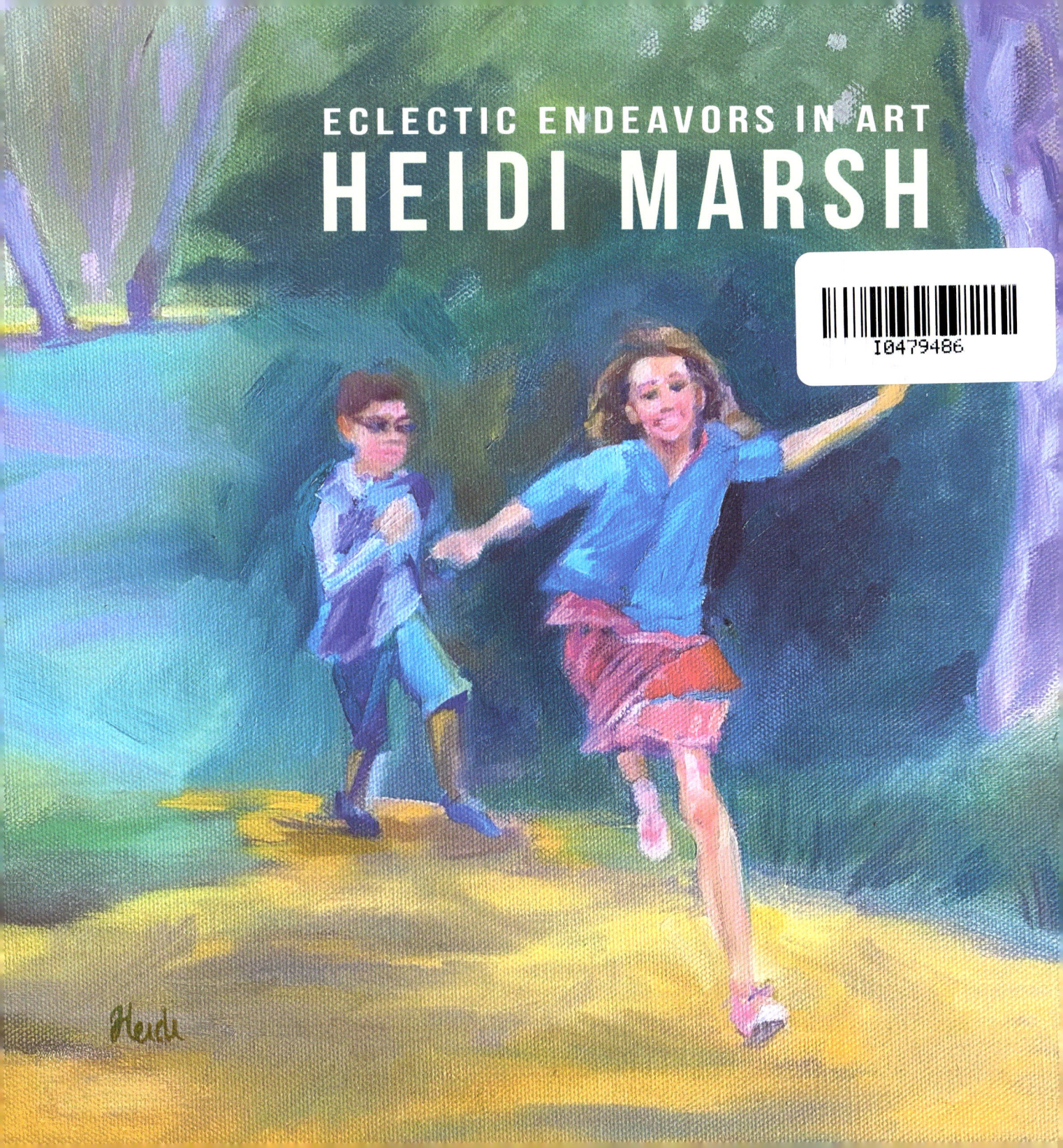

ECLECTIC ENDEAVORS IN ART
HEIDI MARSH

ABOUT THE BOOK:

This book contains artwork inspired from family, pets, other artist's work, and favorite things.

ABOUT ME:

I grew up in Southern California and continue to reside in California with my family. I have been creating art for a substantial part of my life. I remember as a child going to art lessons after school with my friend's mom who was an artist. I also remember taking my art supplies in my red wagon and walking to art lessons a few blocks away at the neighborhood art center.

I enjoyed art so much that I studied it in high school and majored in art at California State University Long Beach where I earned my B.A. in Art degree.

Since college I have enjoyed taking classes mainly at The Art Studio, where I am surrounded by my artist friends. I have used different mediums with my favorite being oil paints.

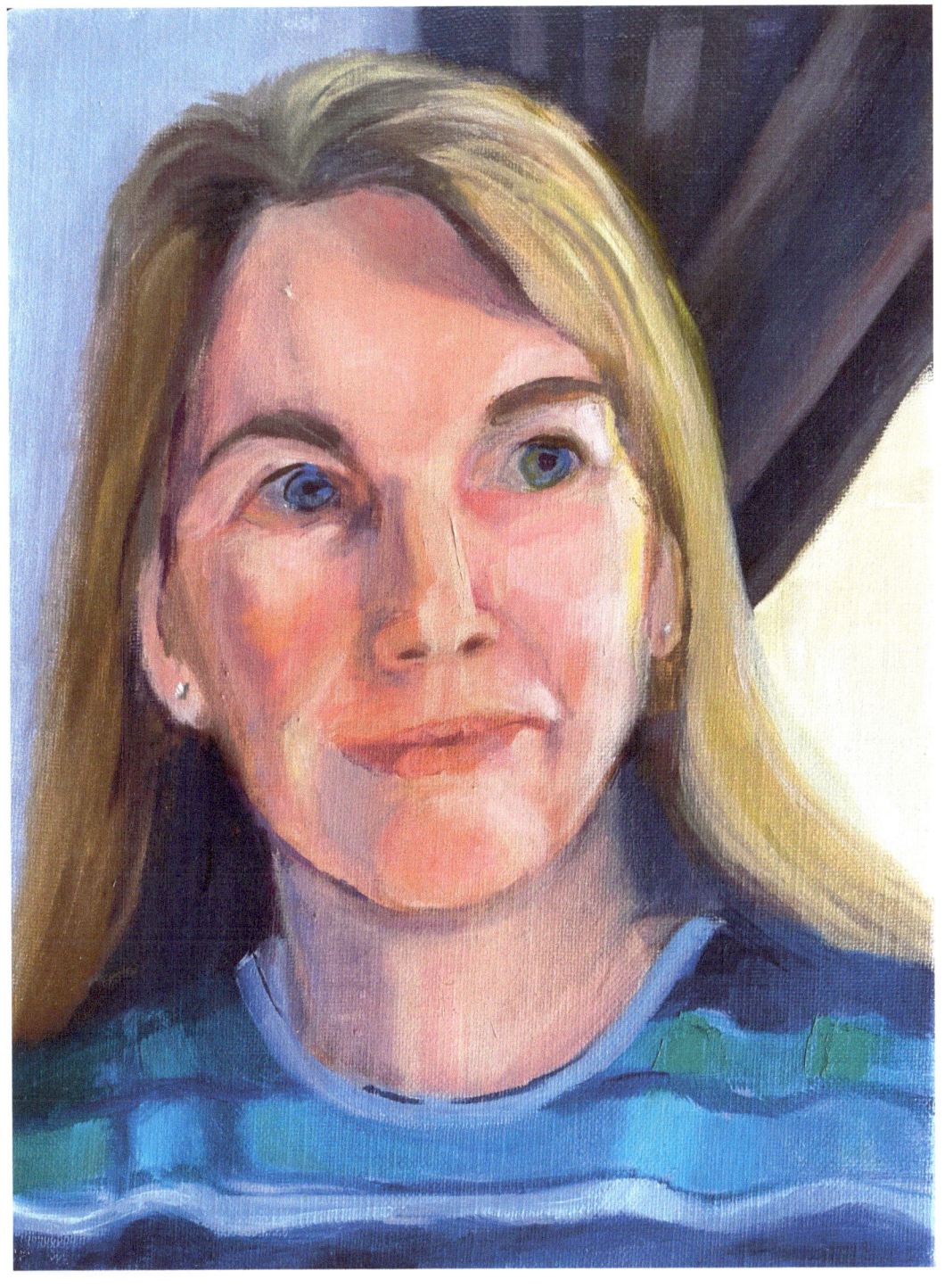

DEDICATION:

I dedicate this book to my loving husband Derek. He has always encouraged and supported me in my artistic endeavors for the 32 years we have been married. I am eternally grateful to him for his love and continued support.

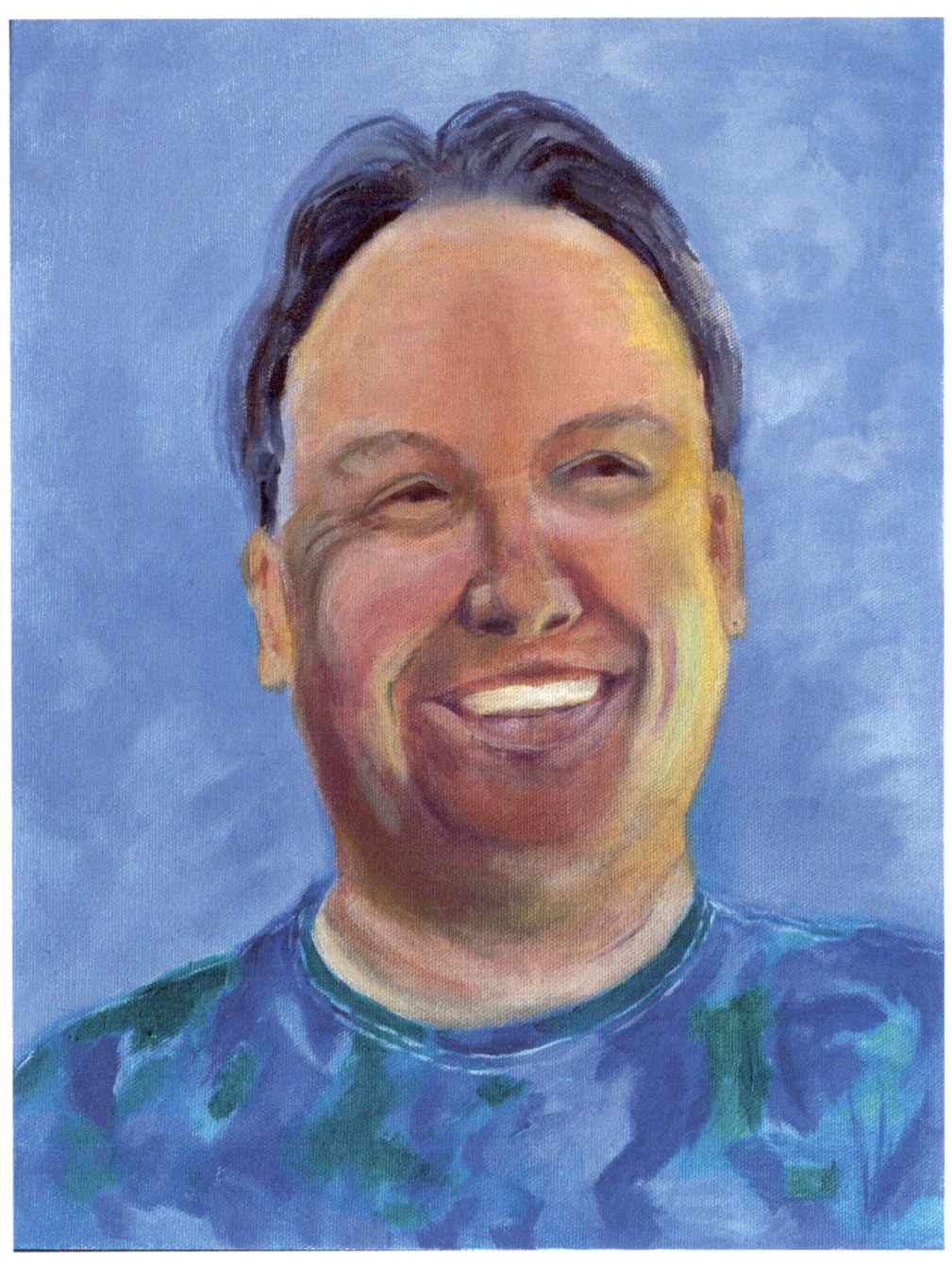

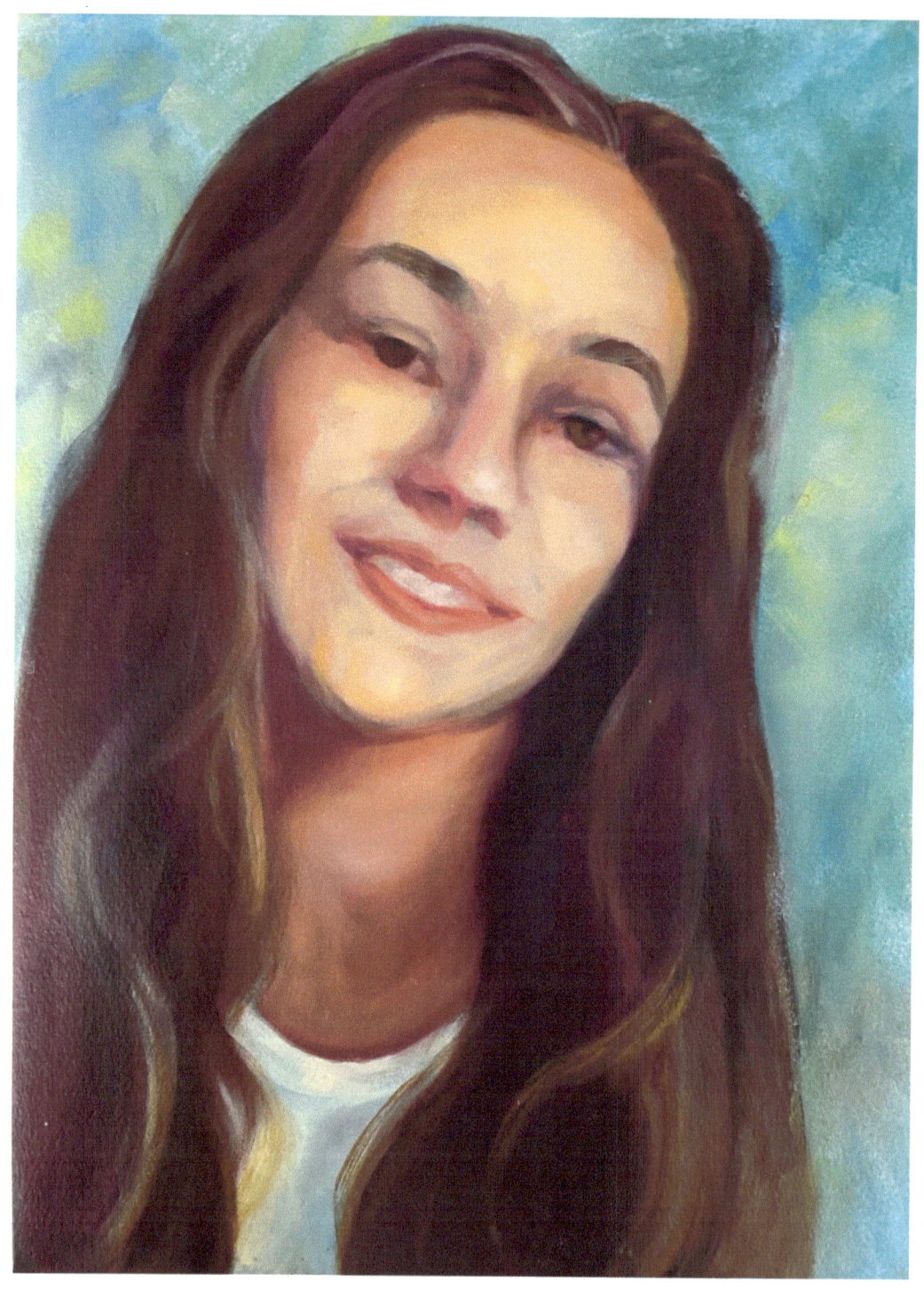

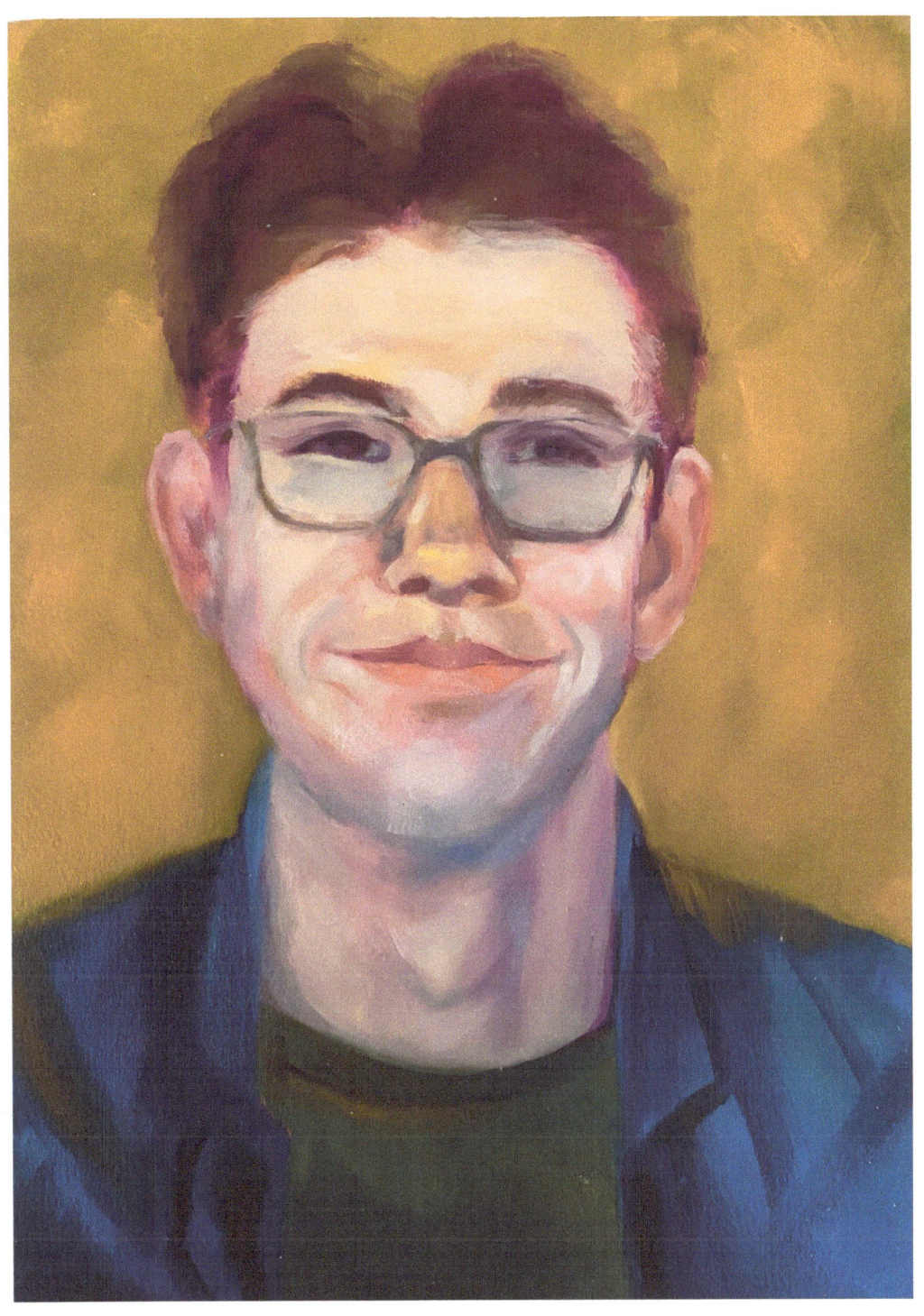

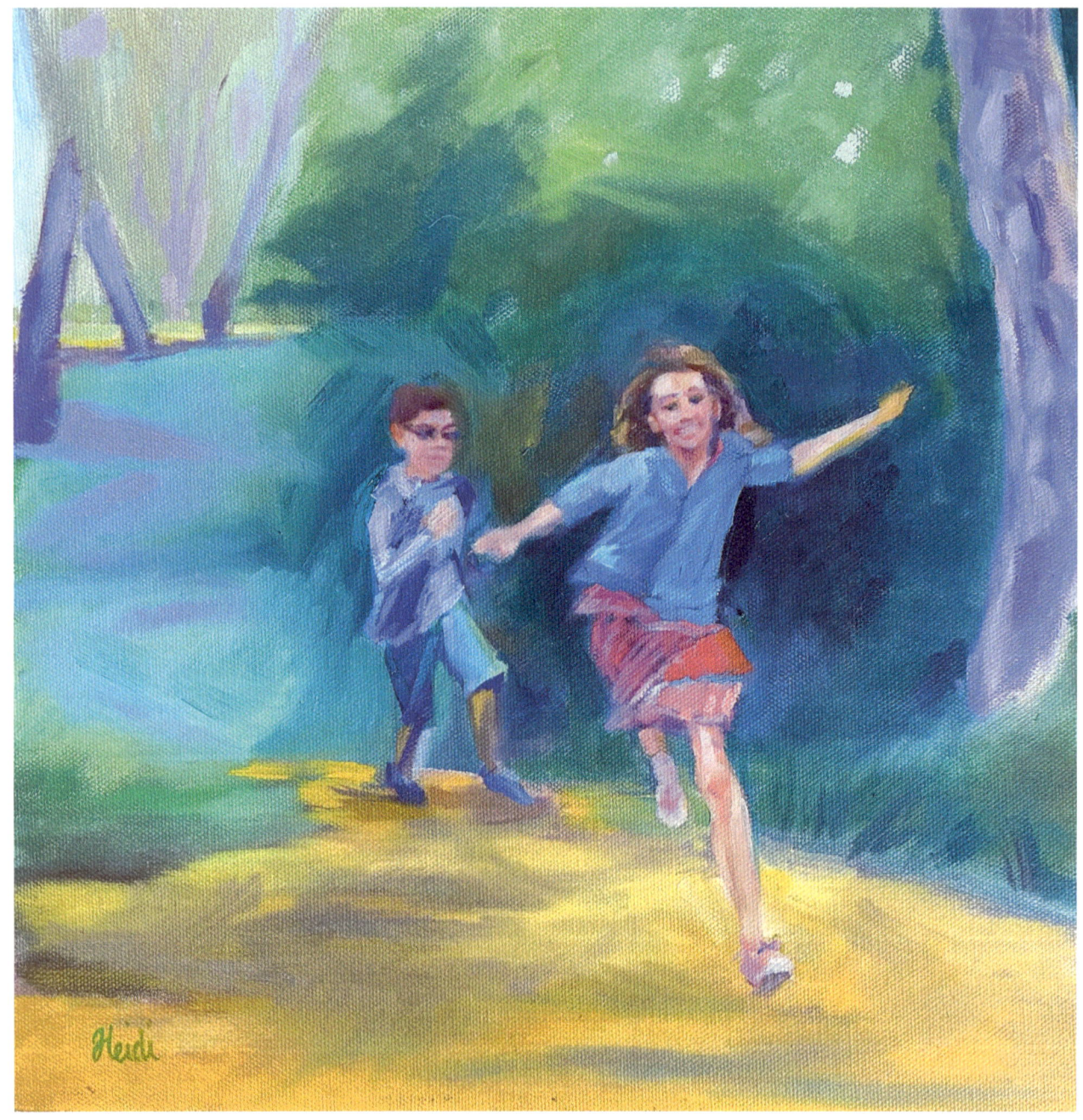

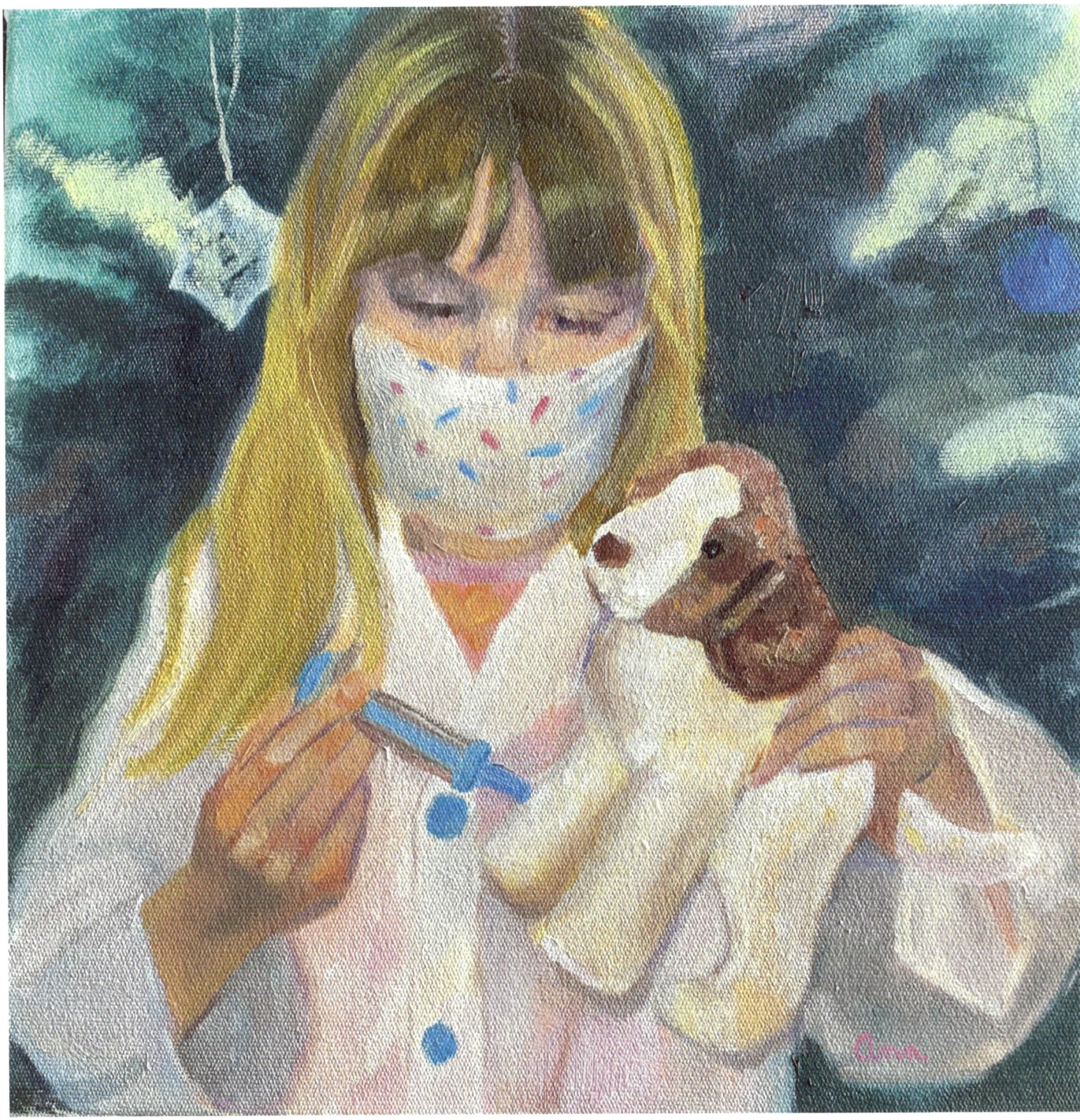

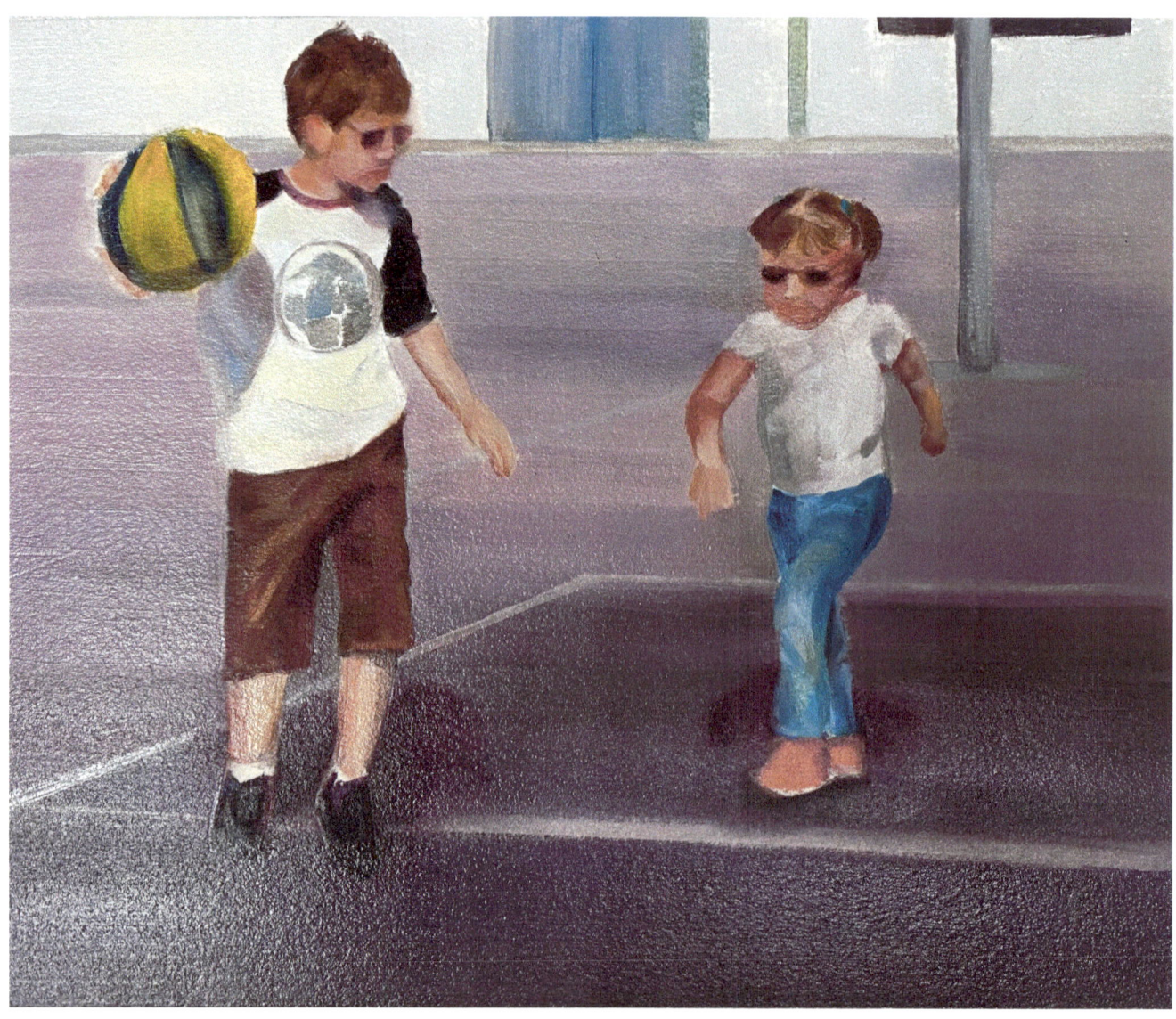

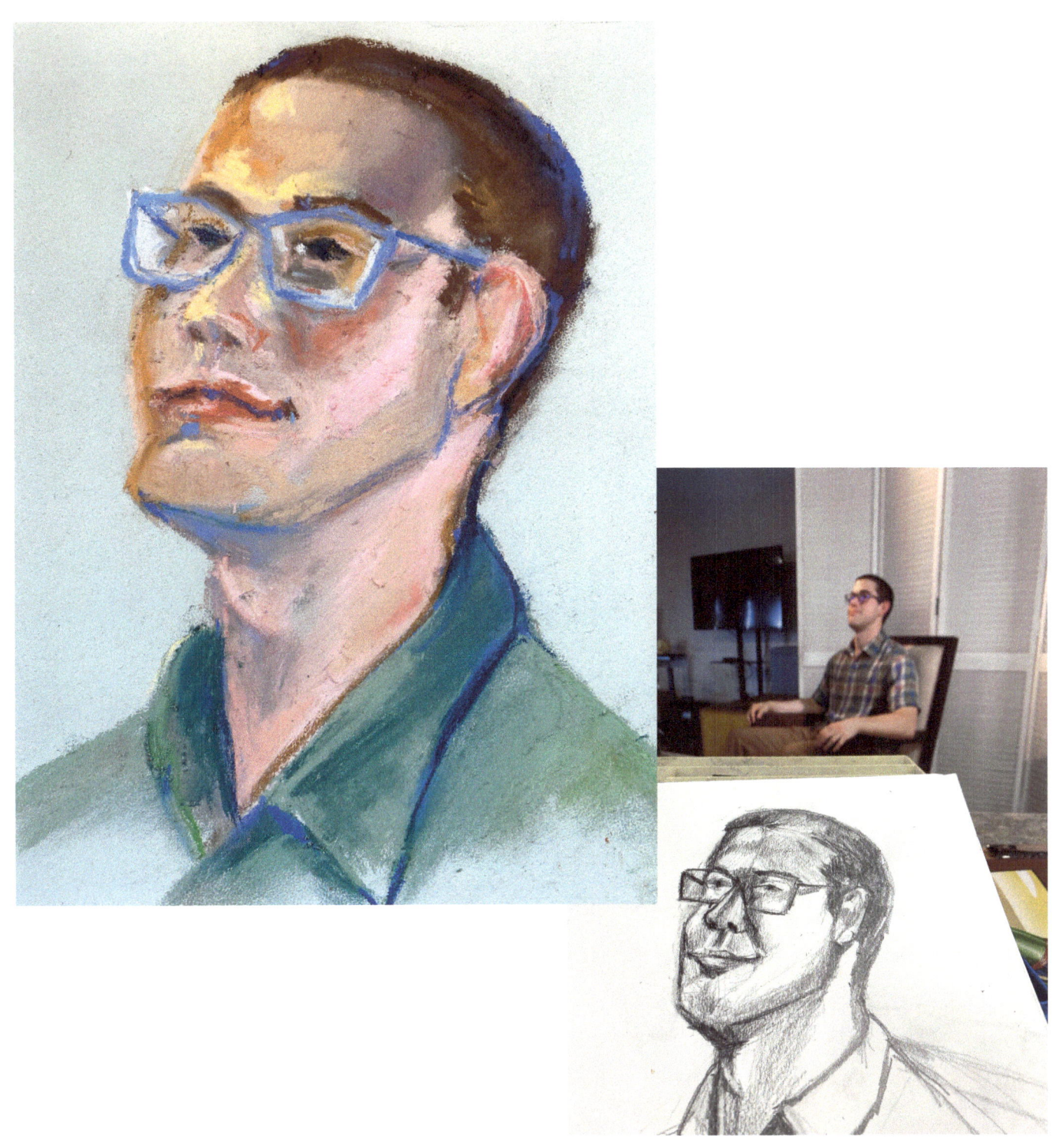

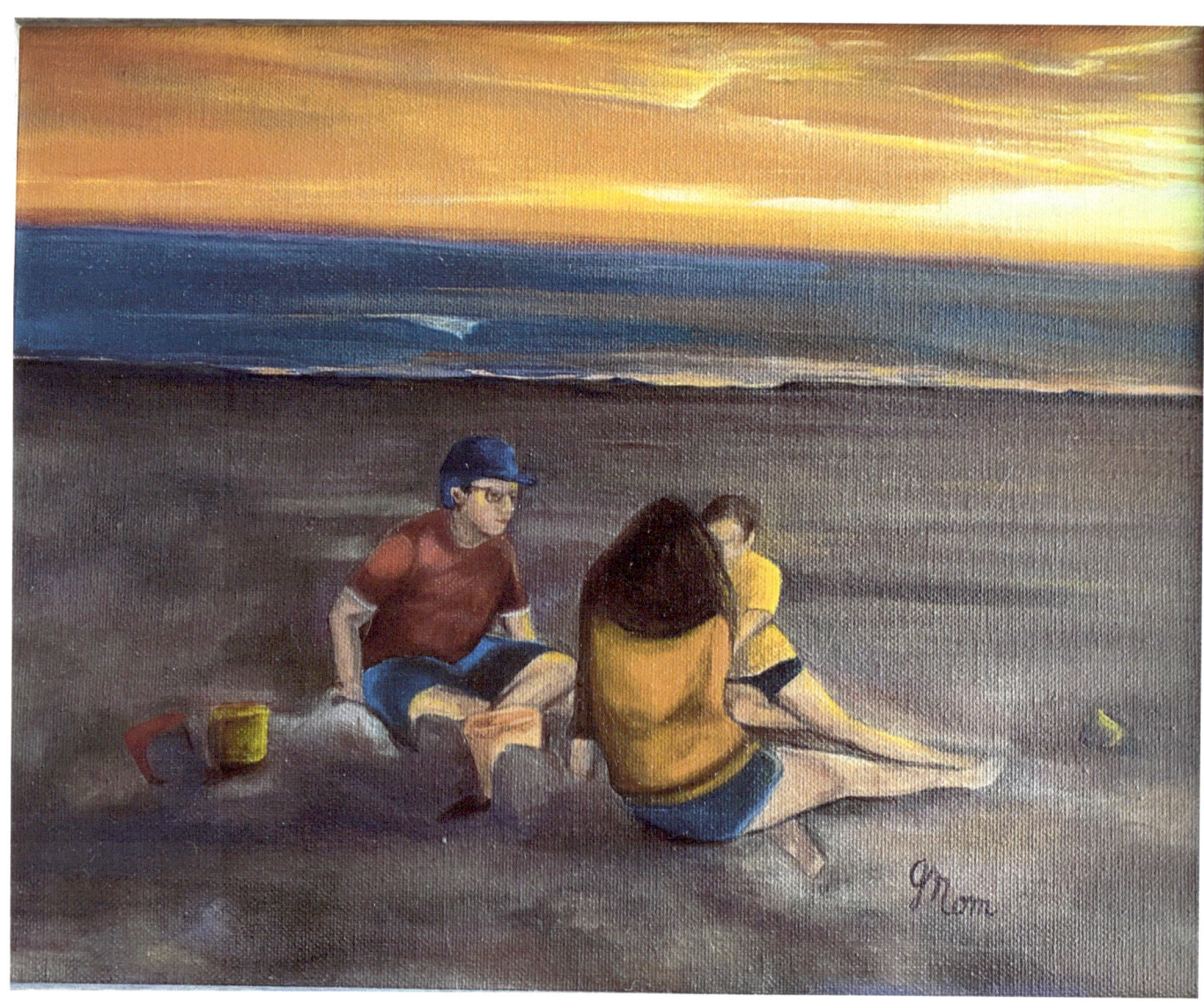

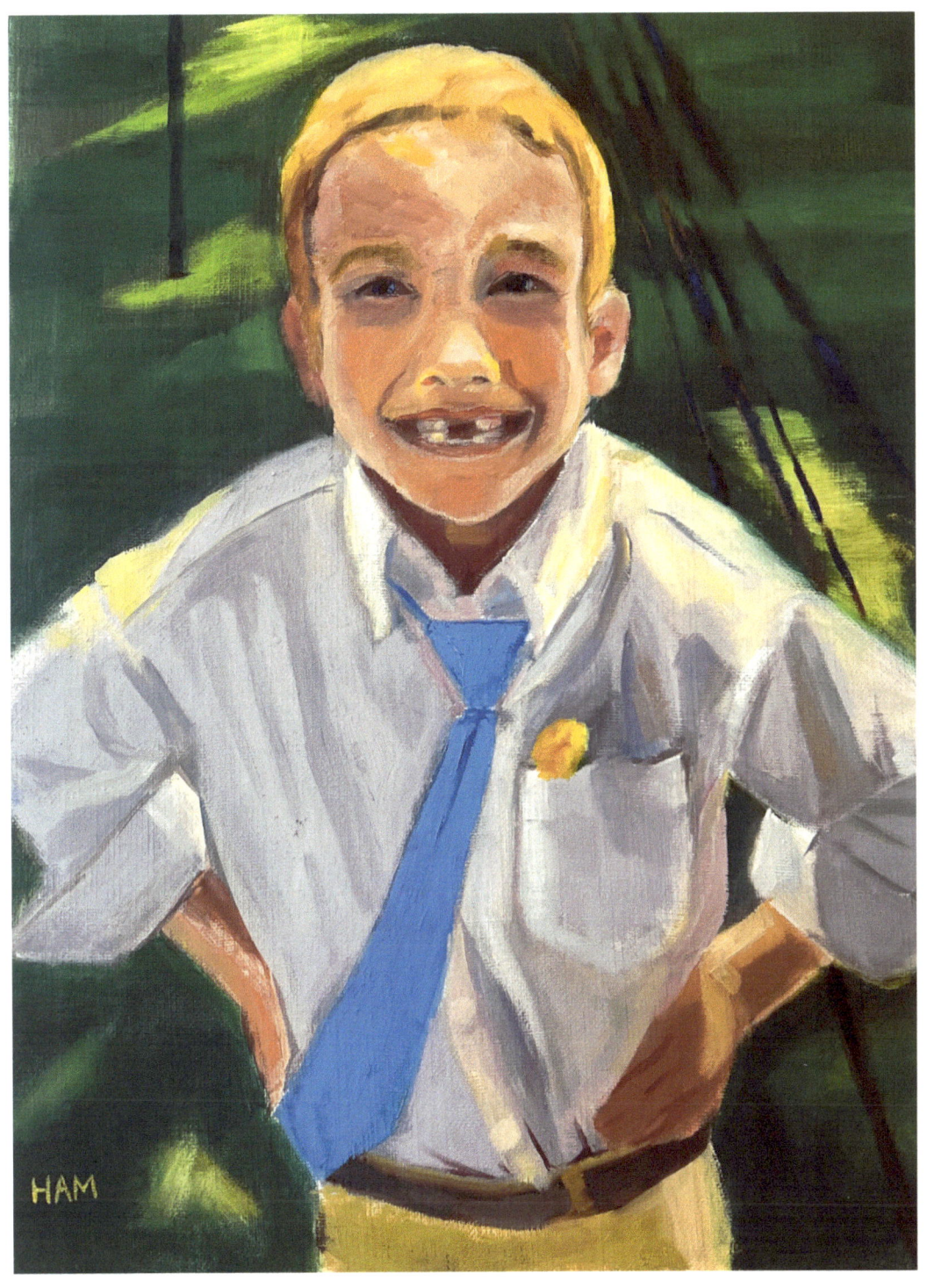

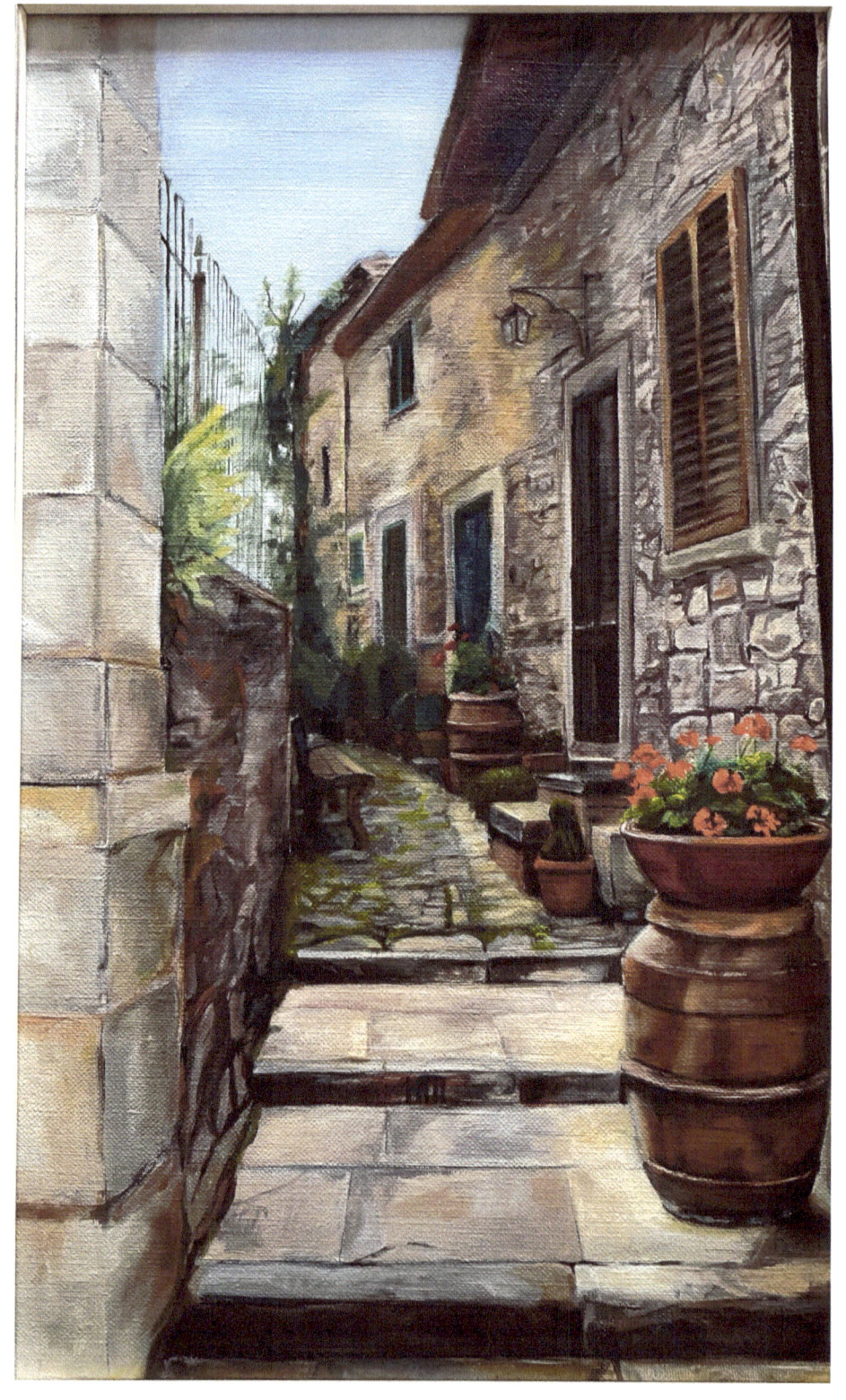

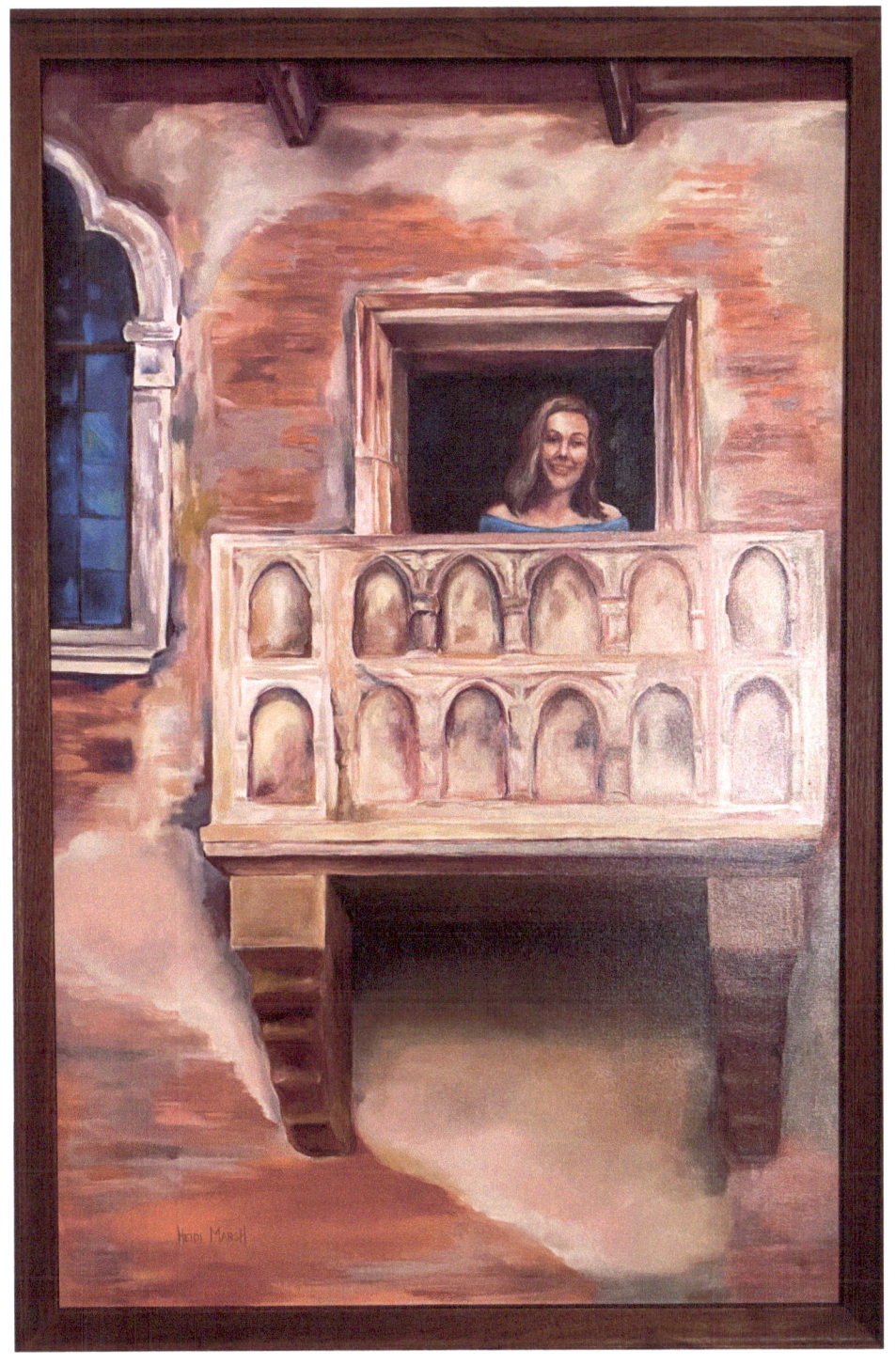

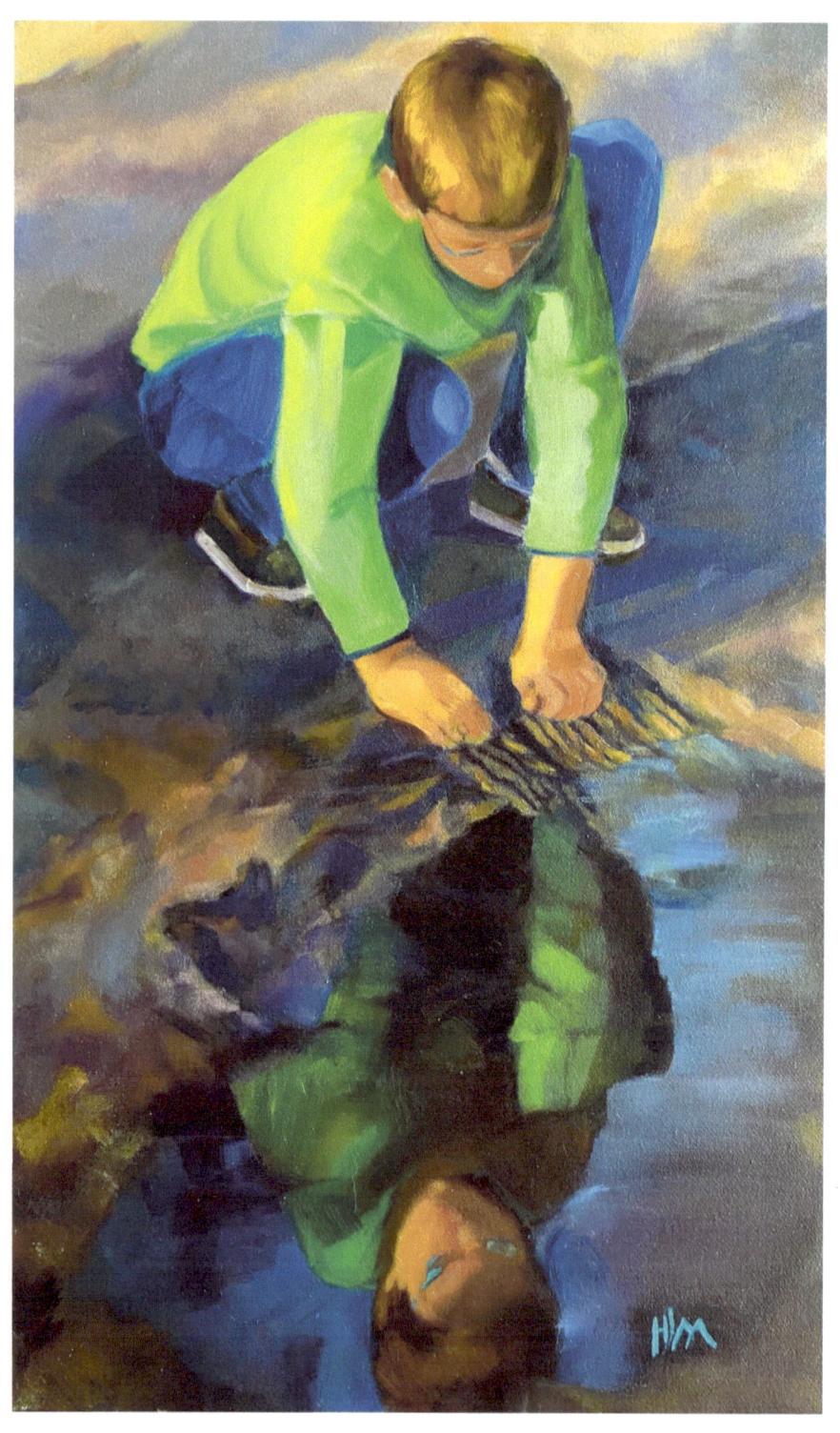

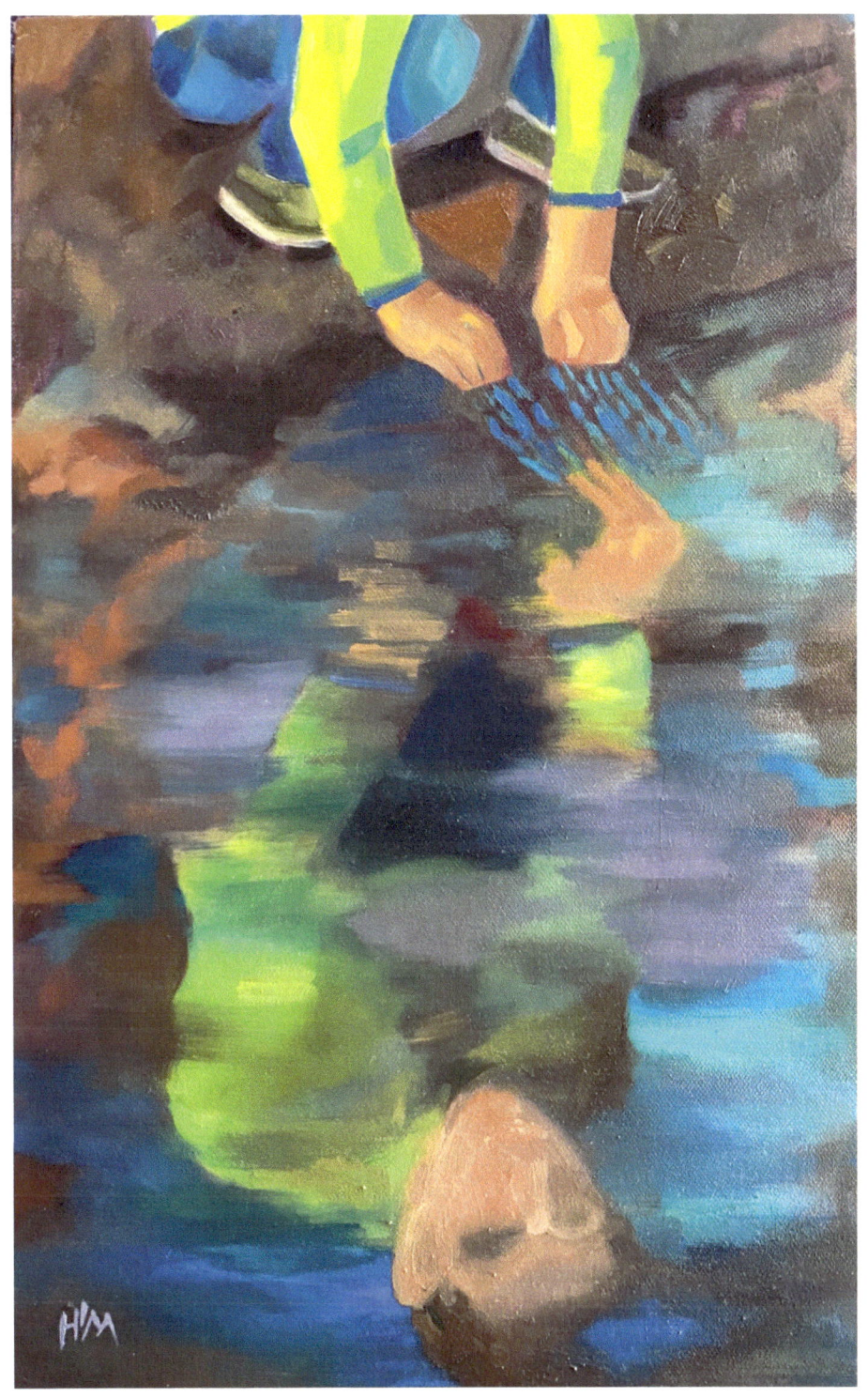

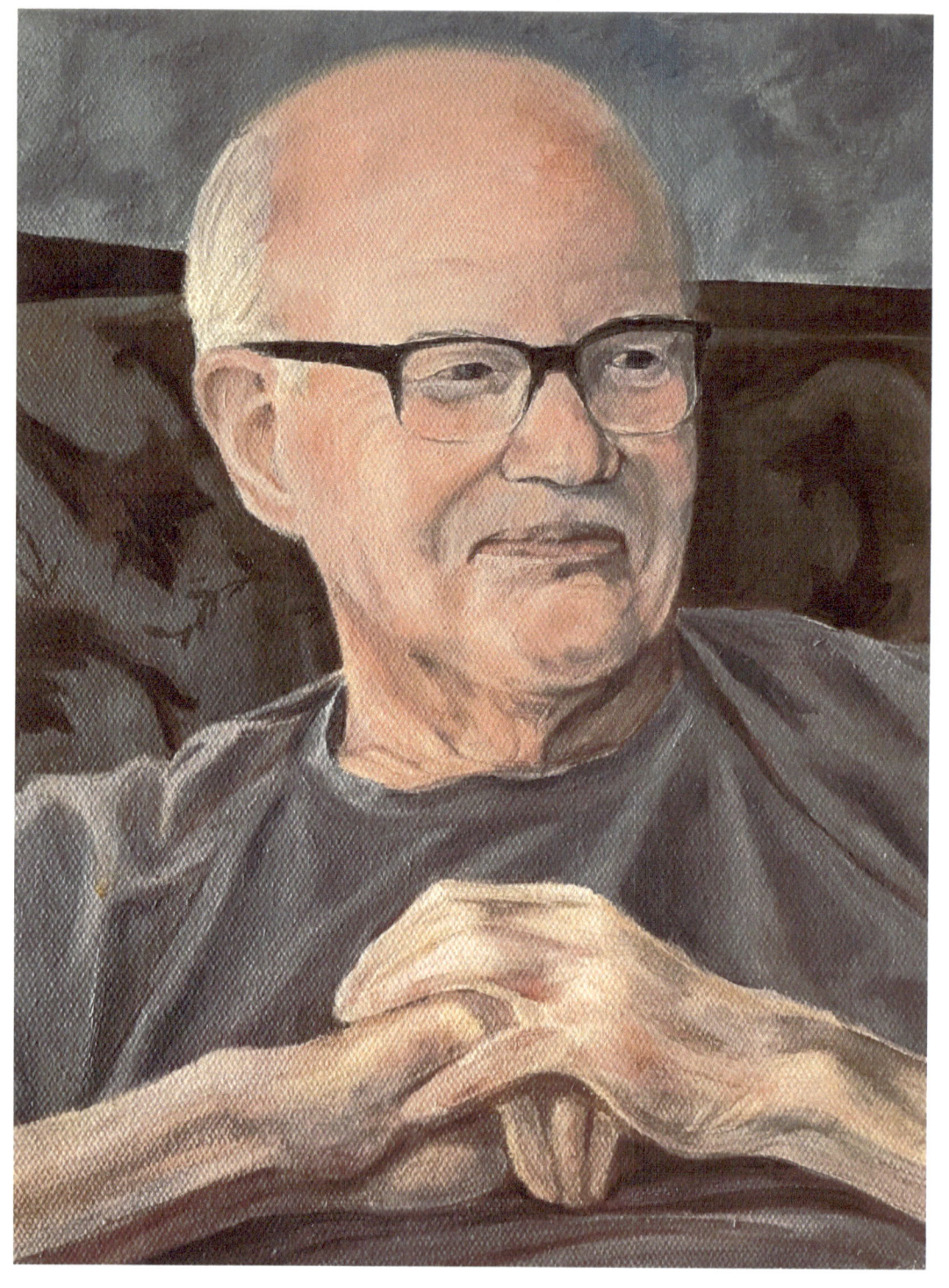

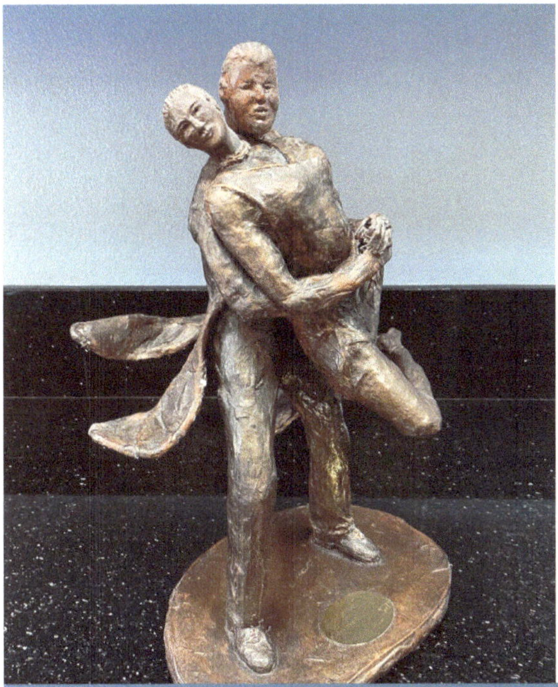

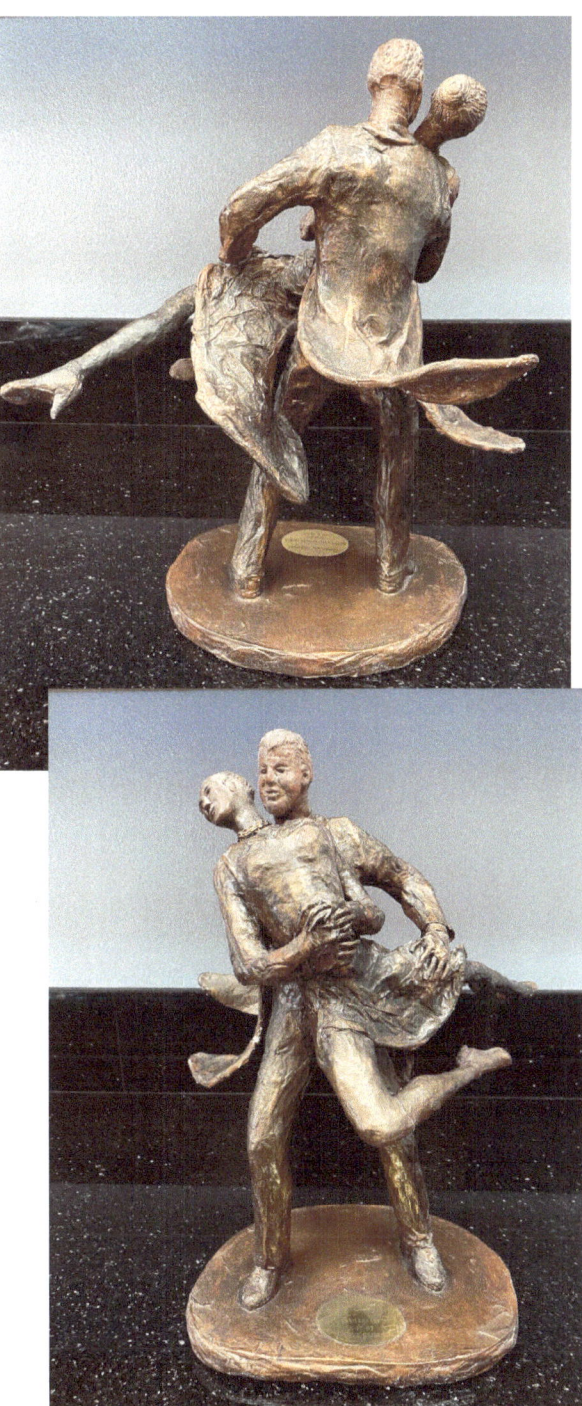

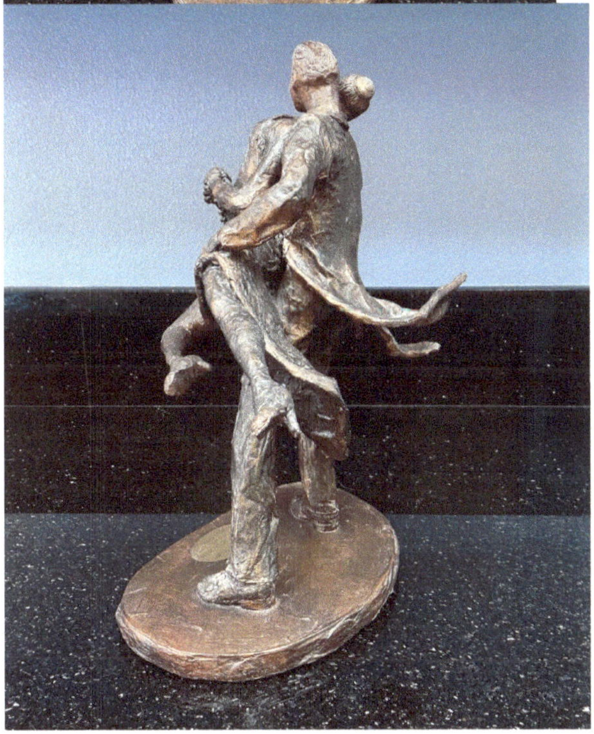

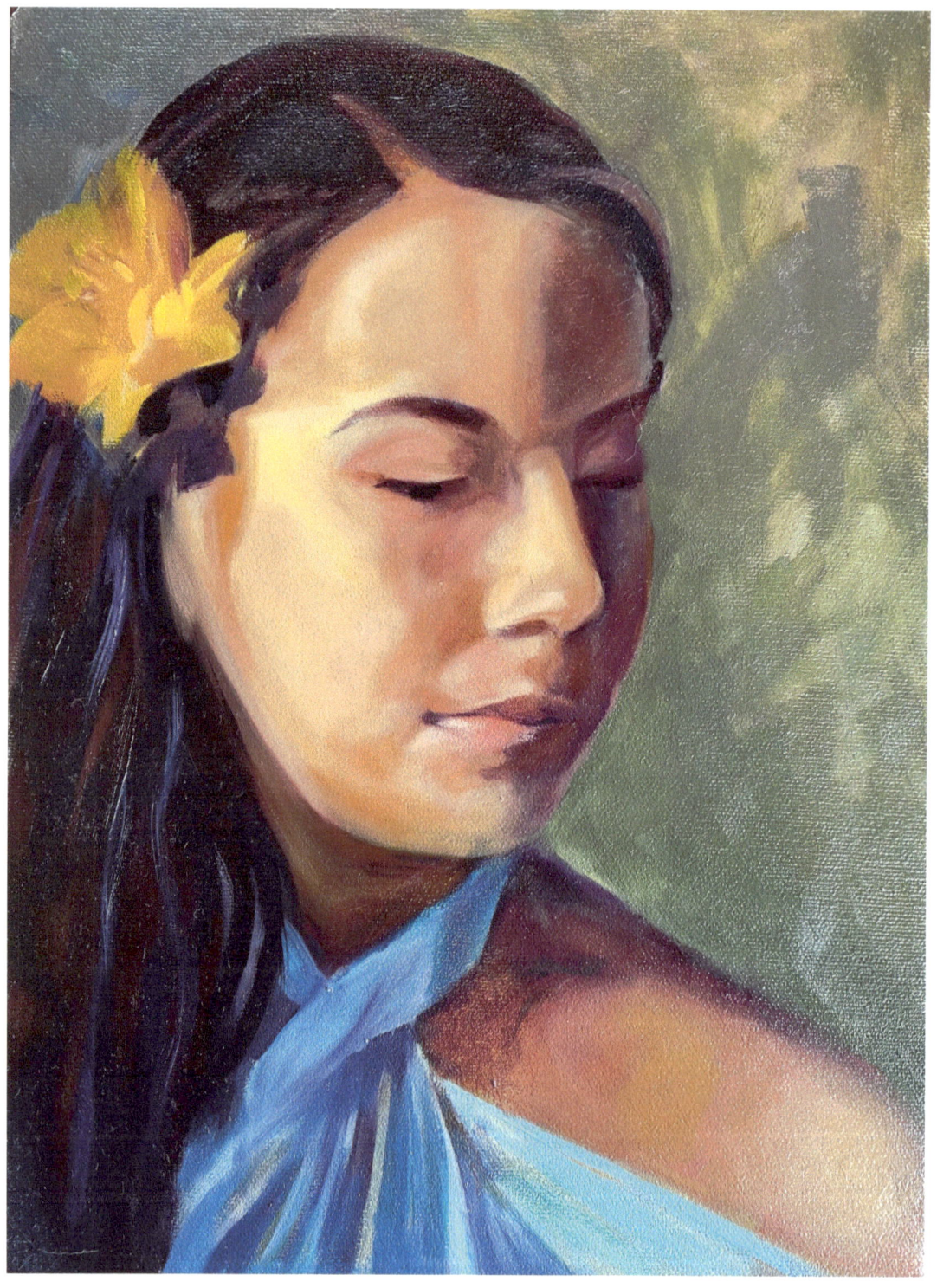

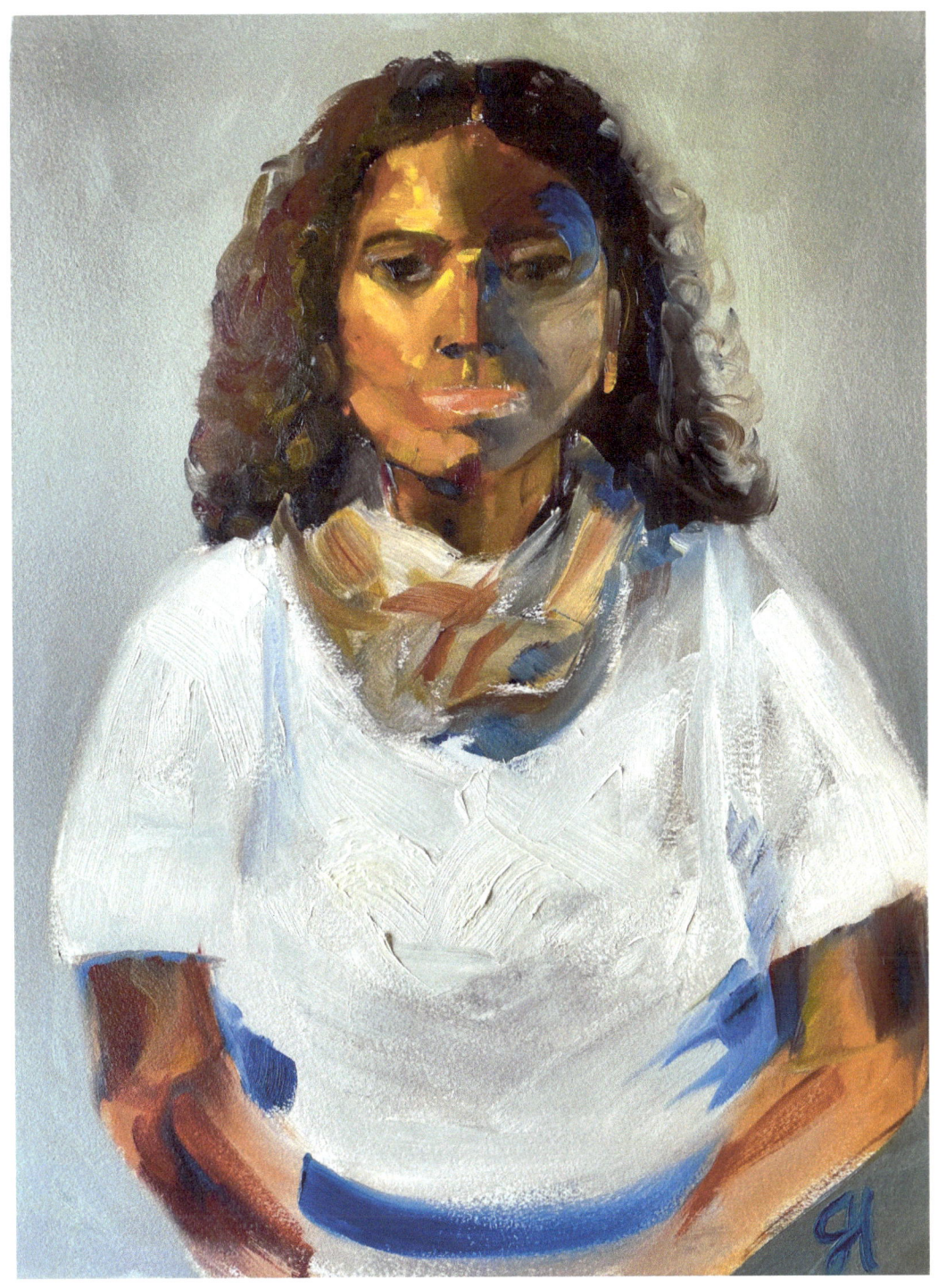

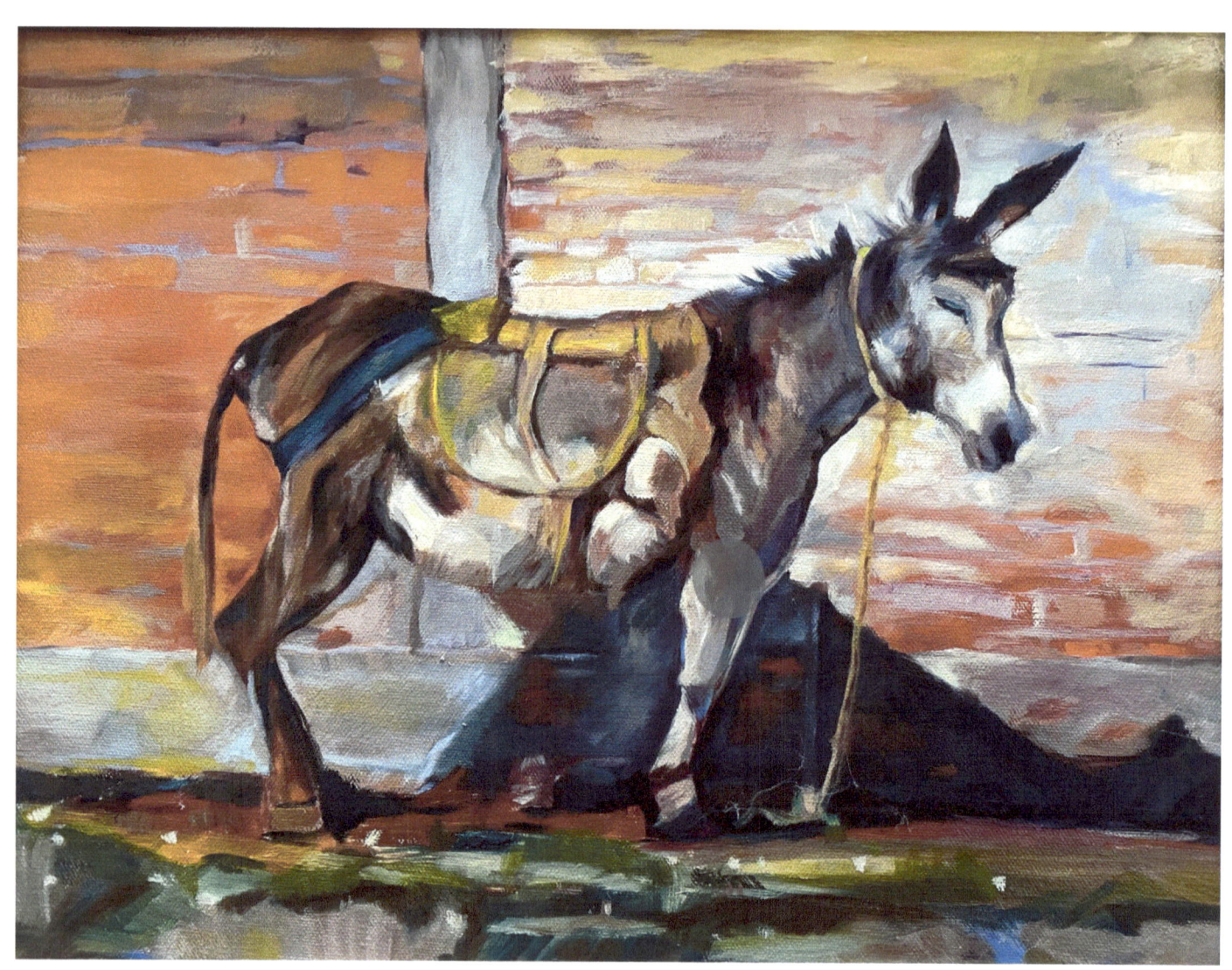

Based on painting by Irby Brown

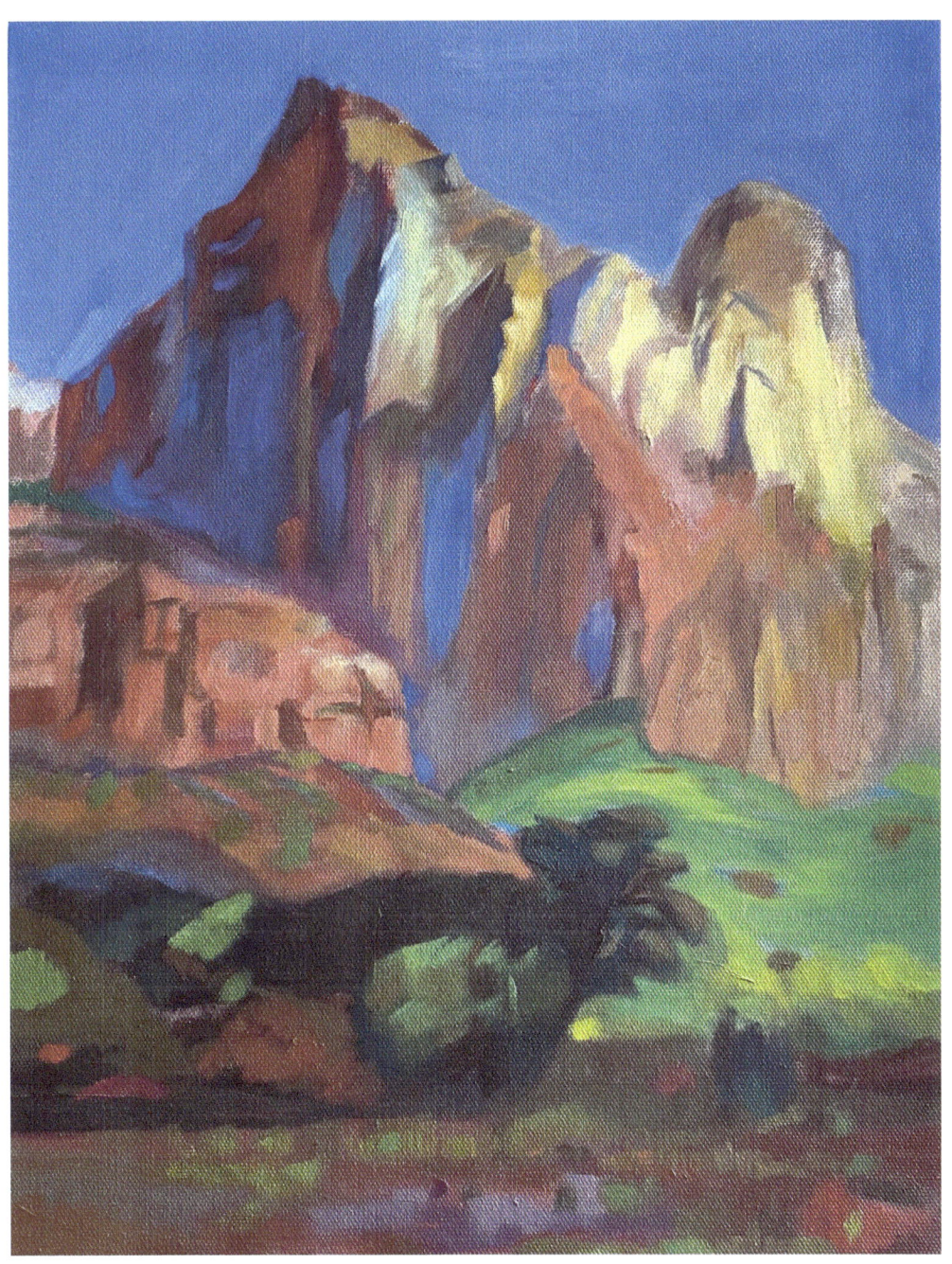

PAINTING STUDY OF FRANZ A. BISCHOFF MOUNTAINS

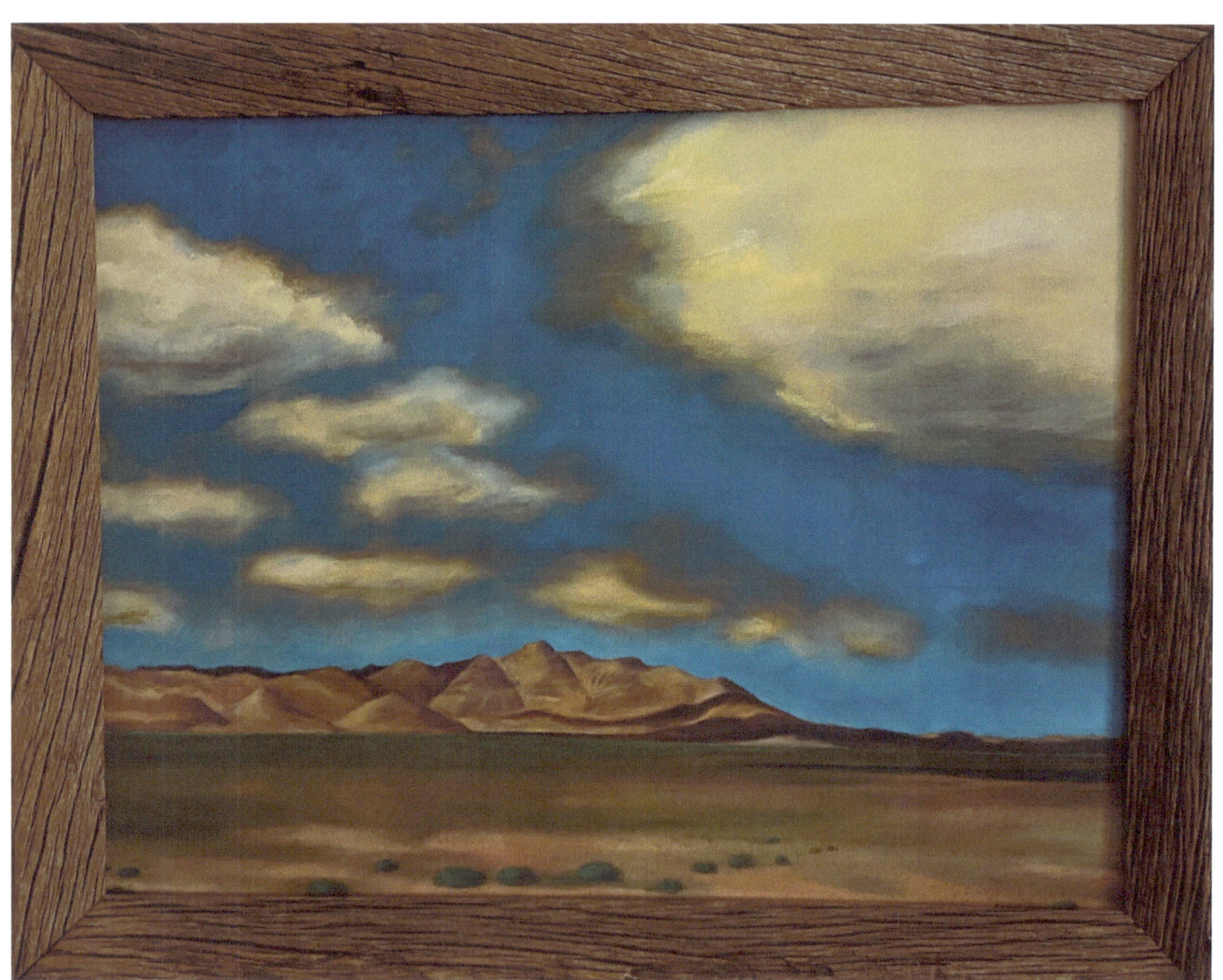

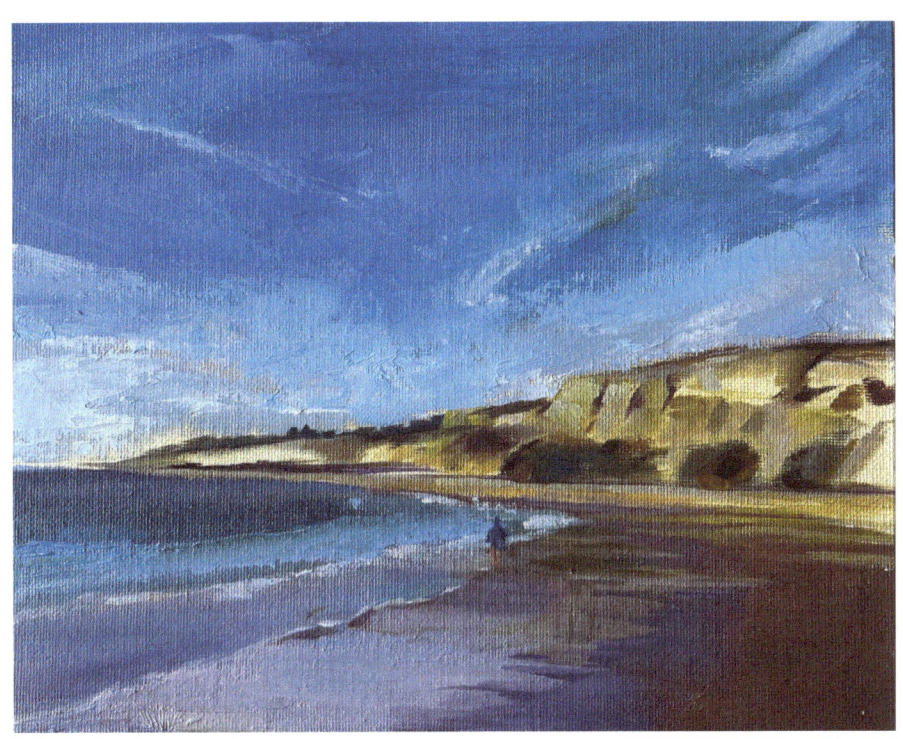

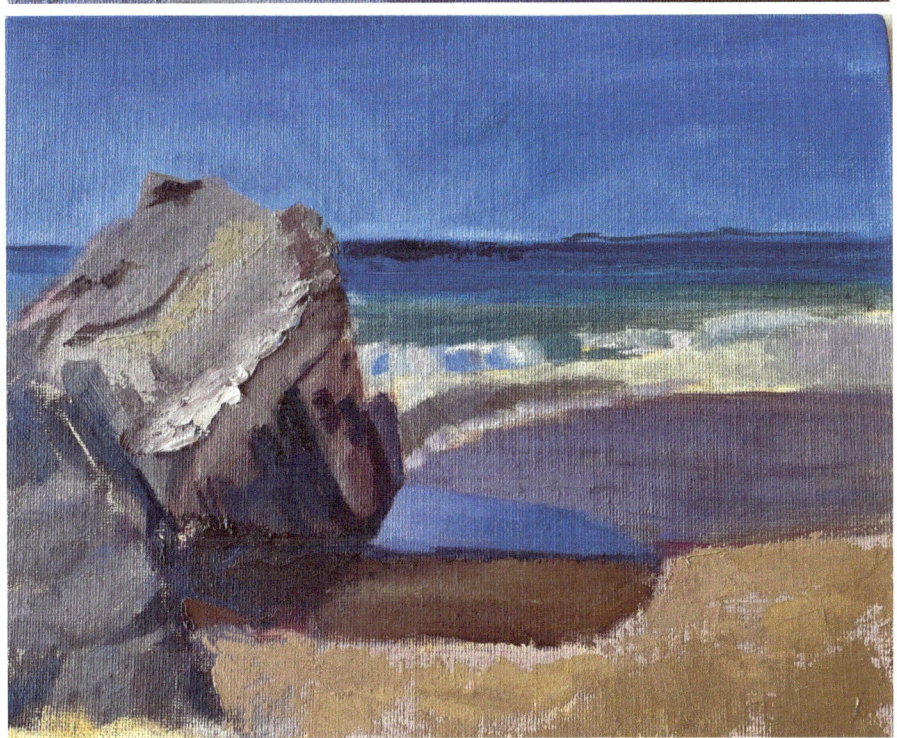

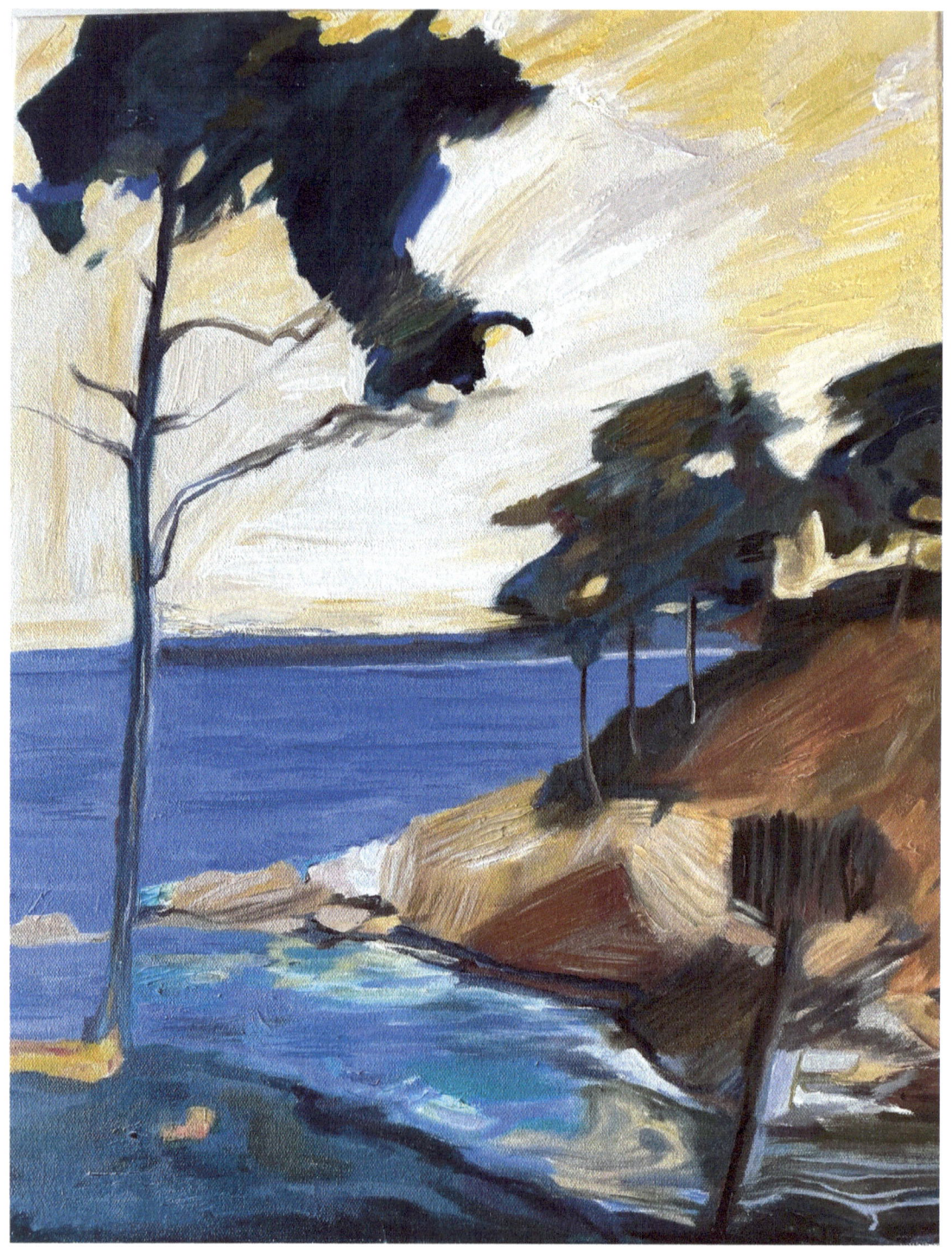

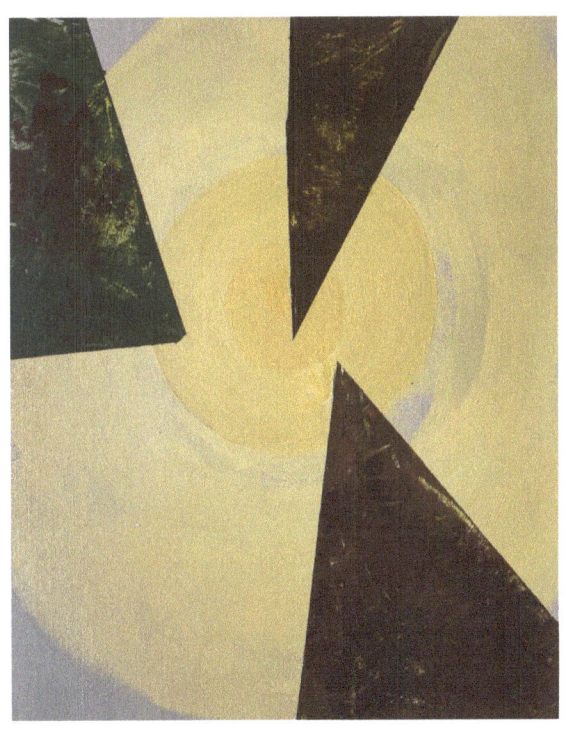
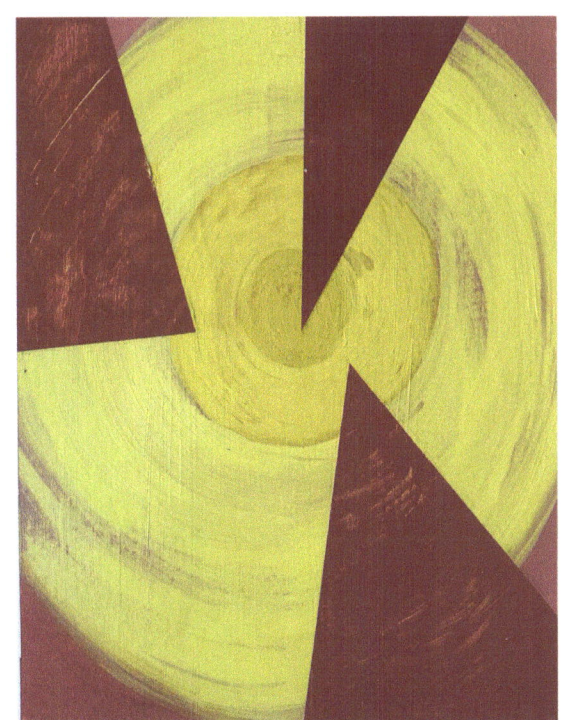
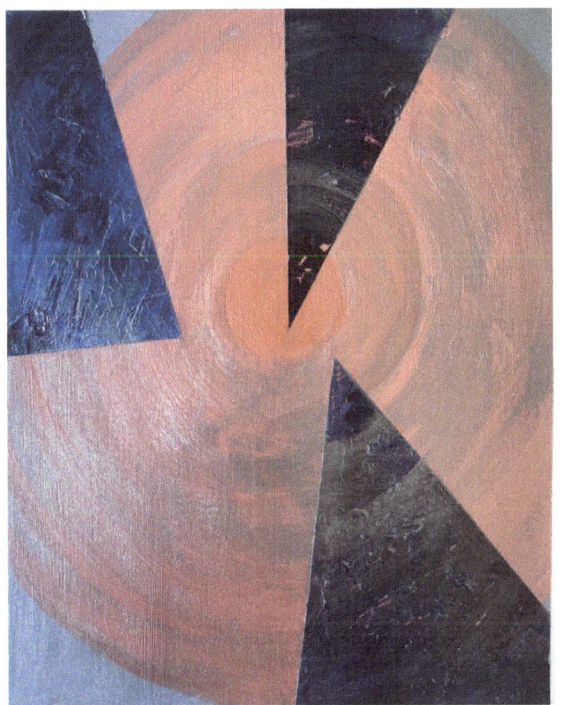
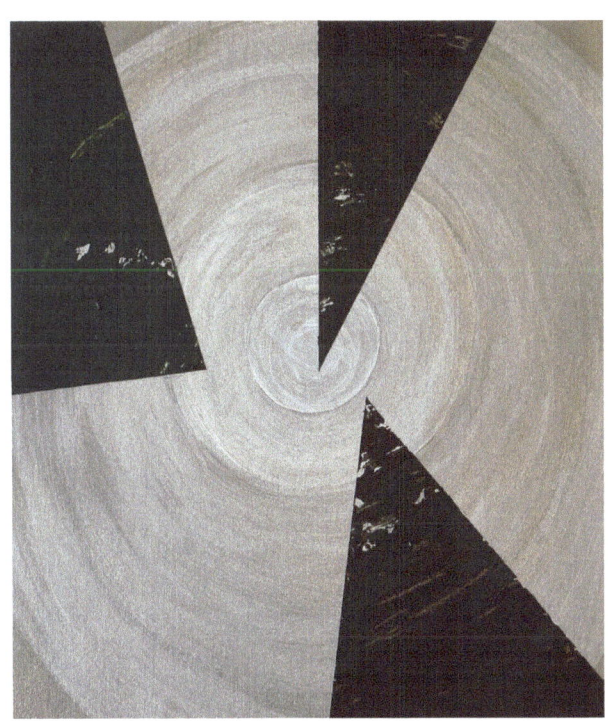

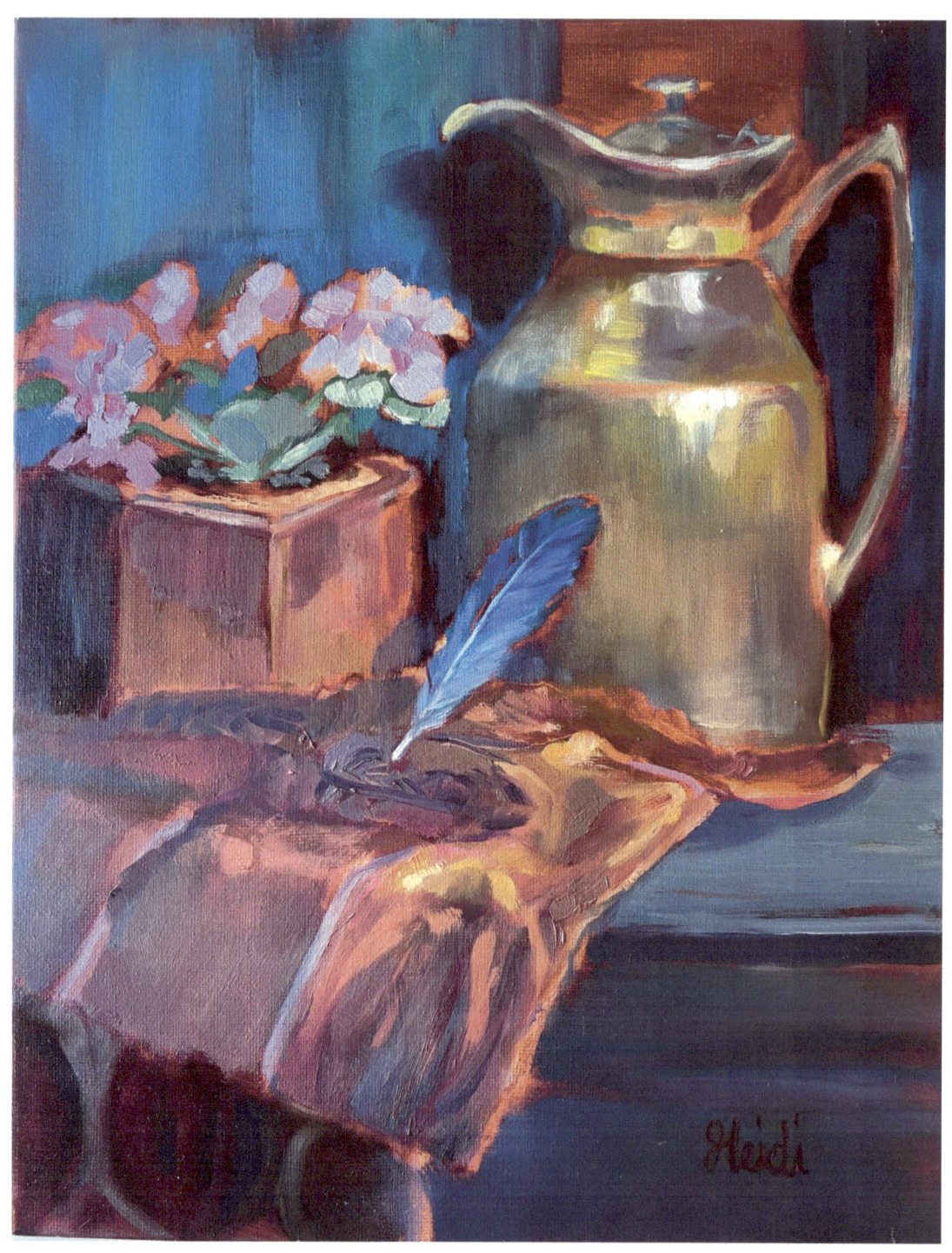

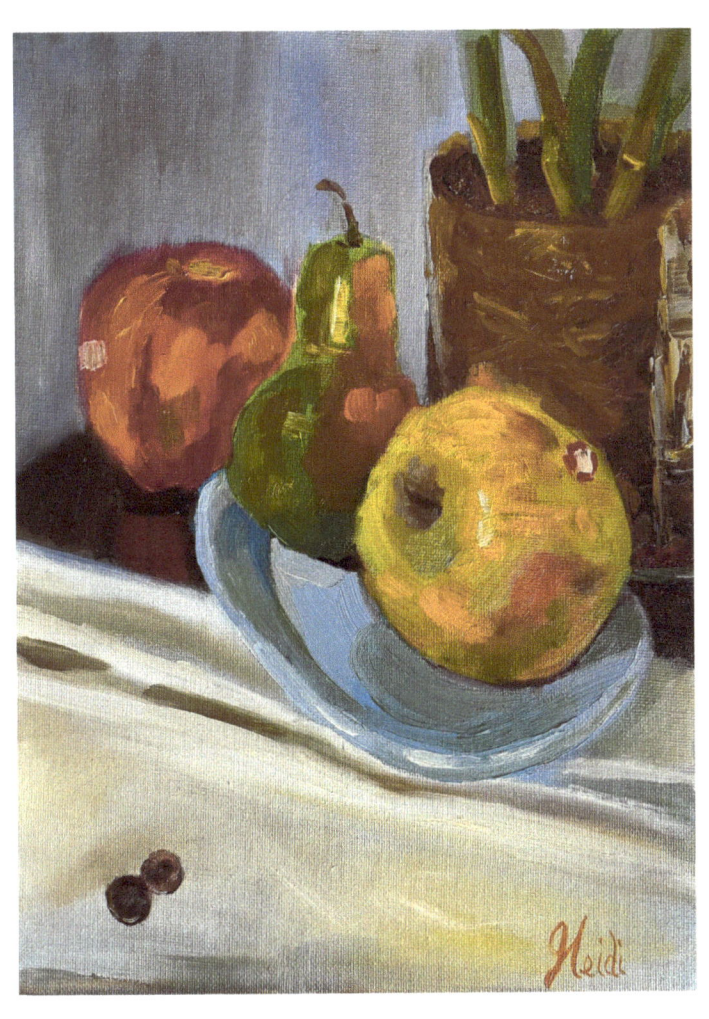

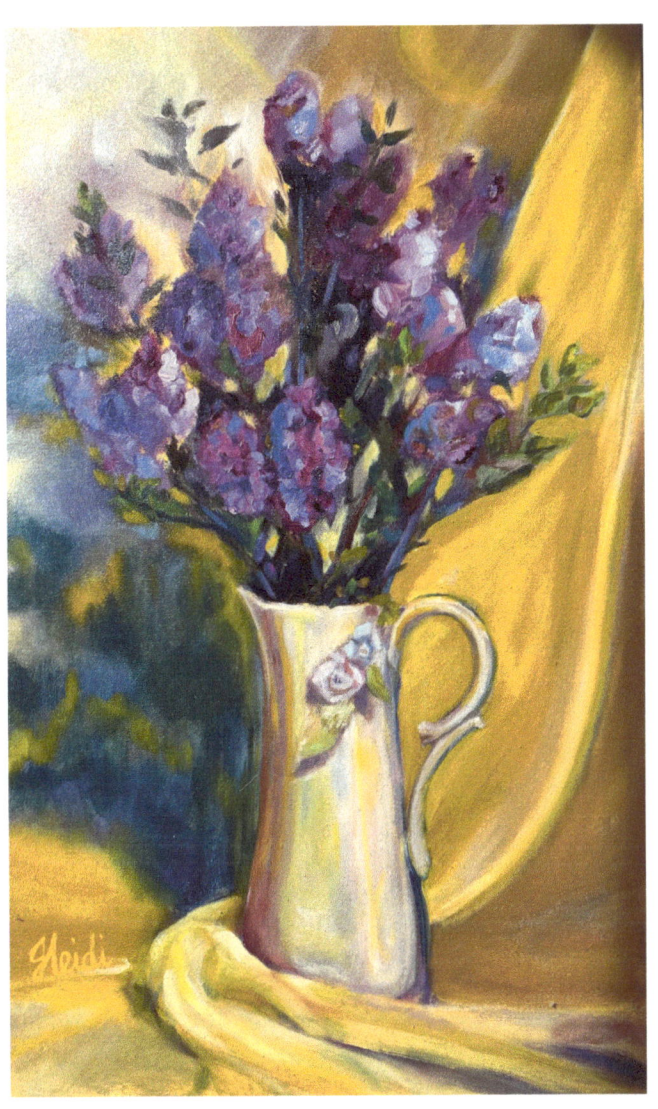

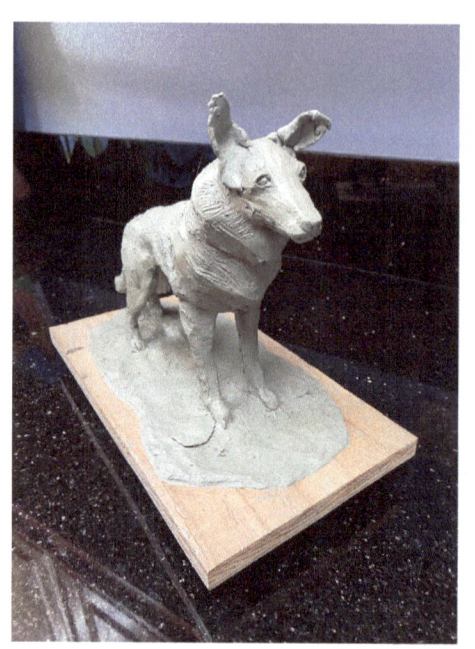

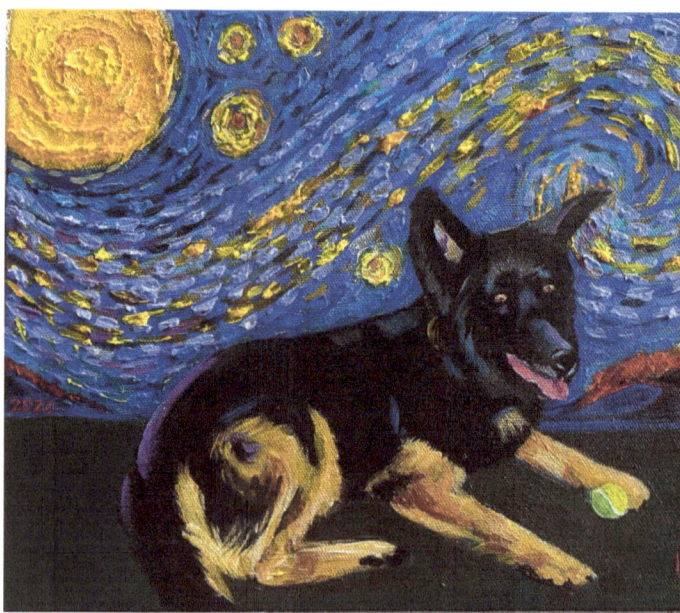

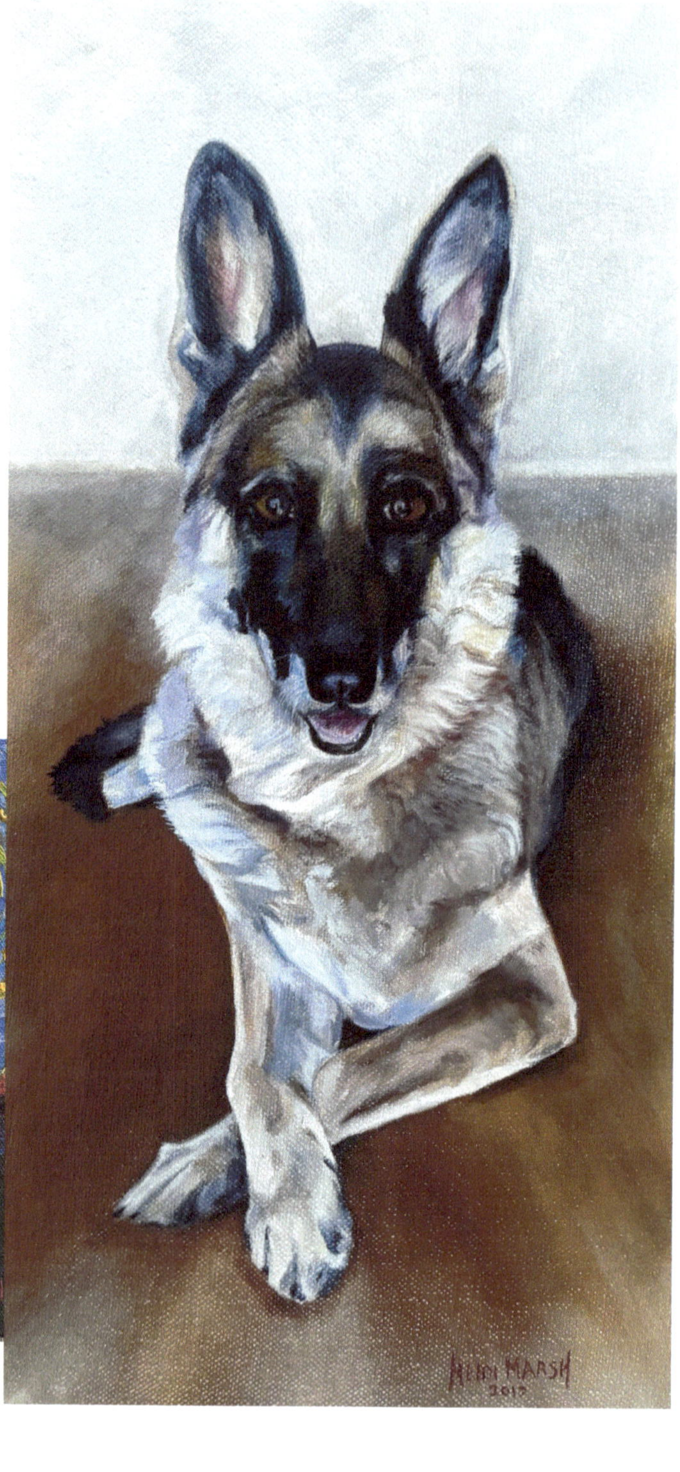

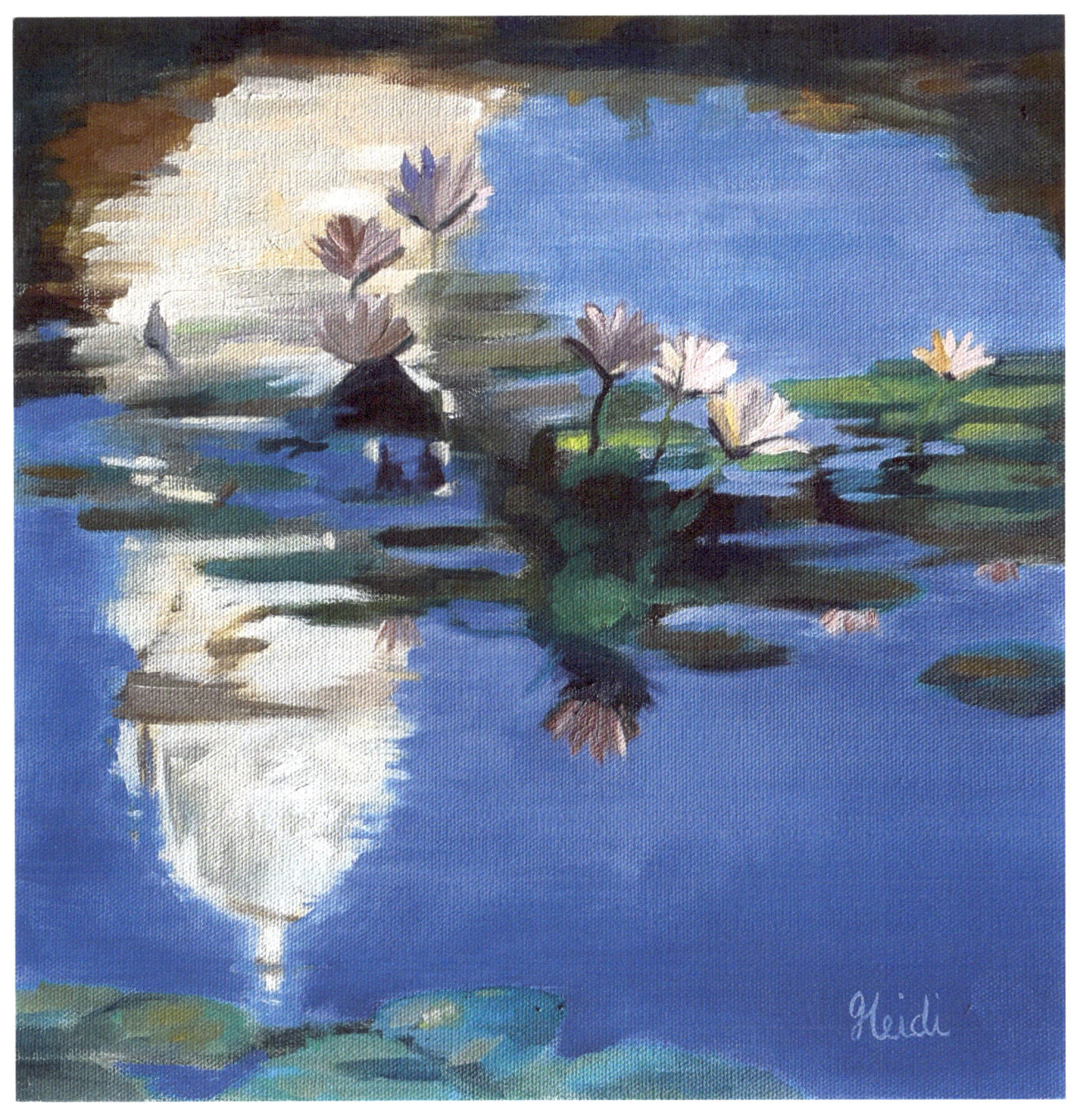

PAINTING STUDY OF BILLUPS WATER LILLIES

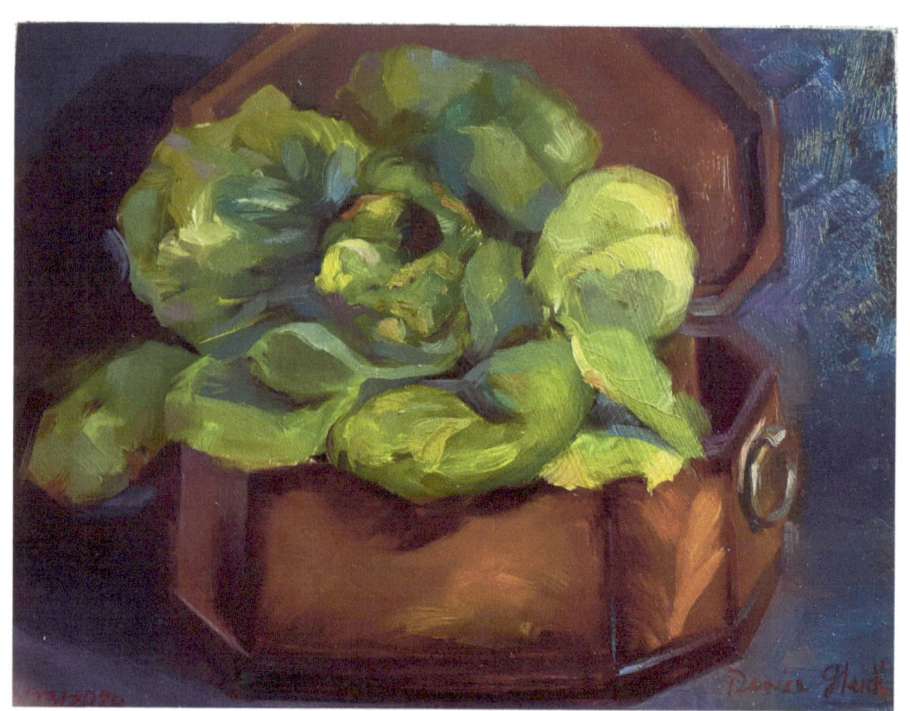

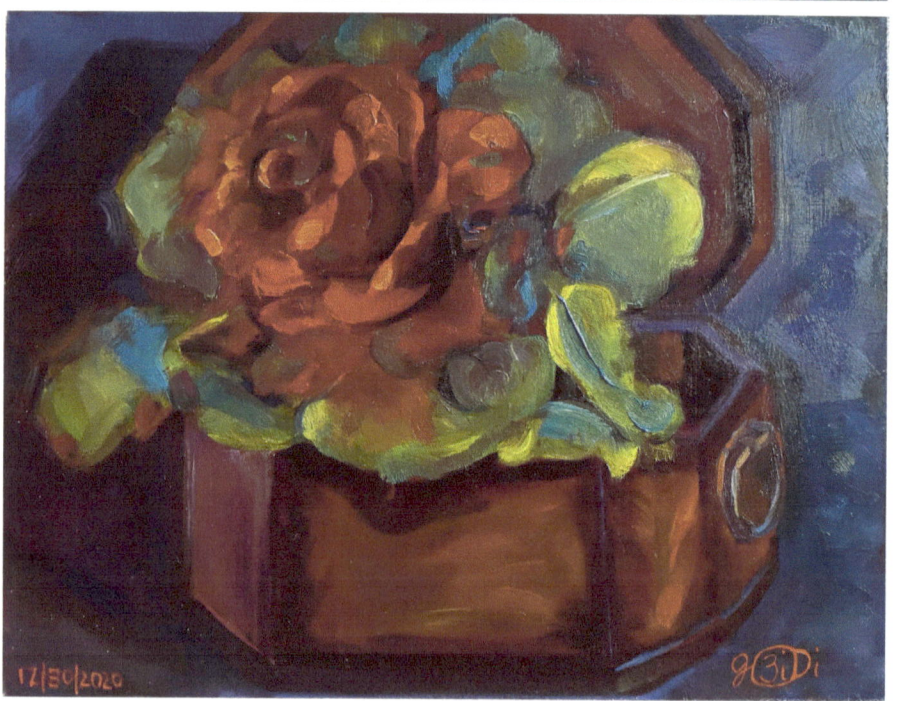

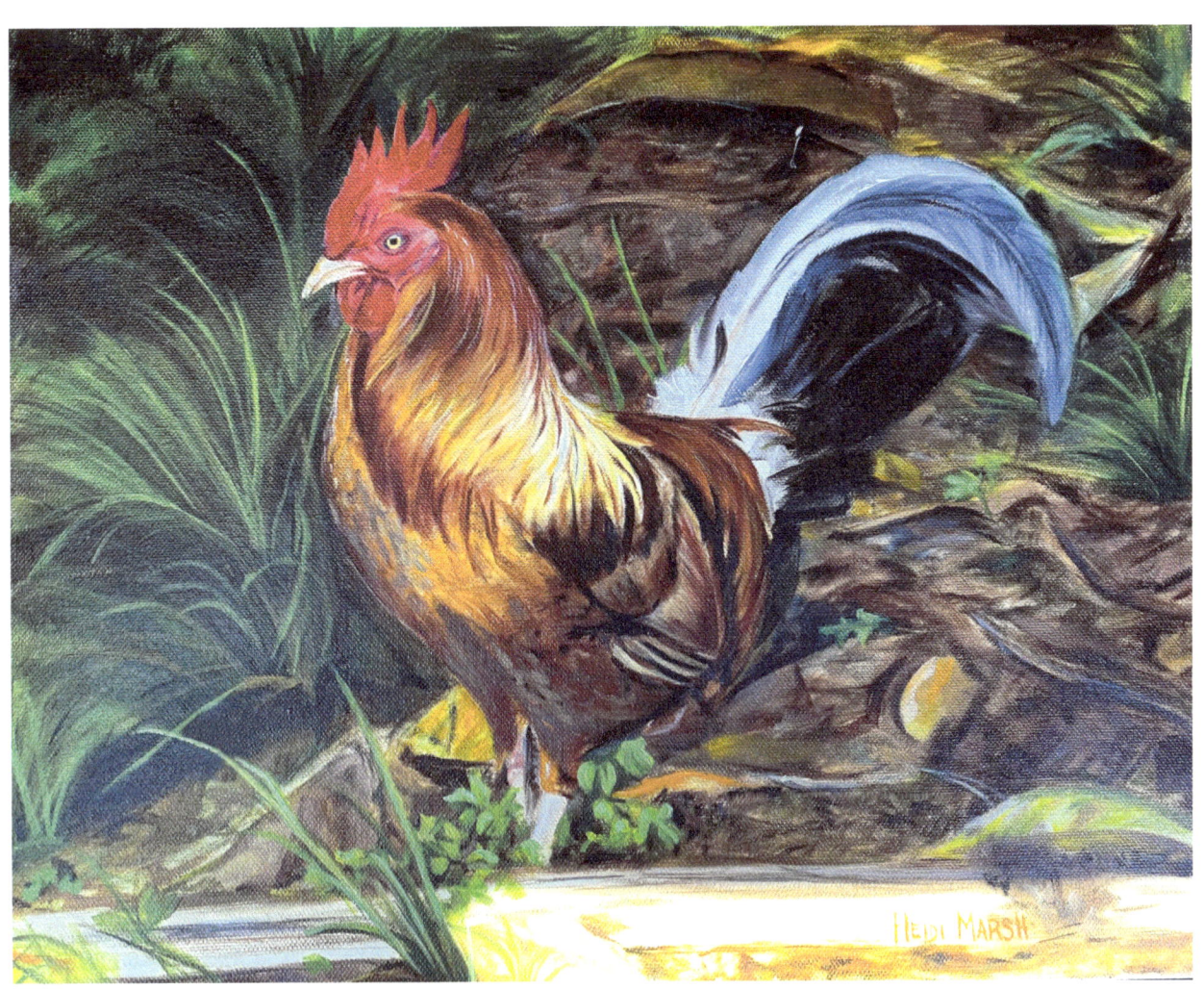
Heidi Marsh

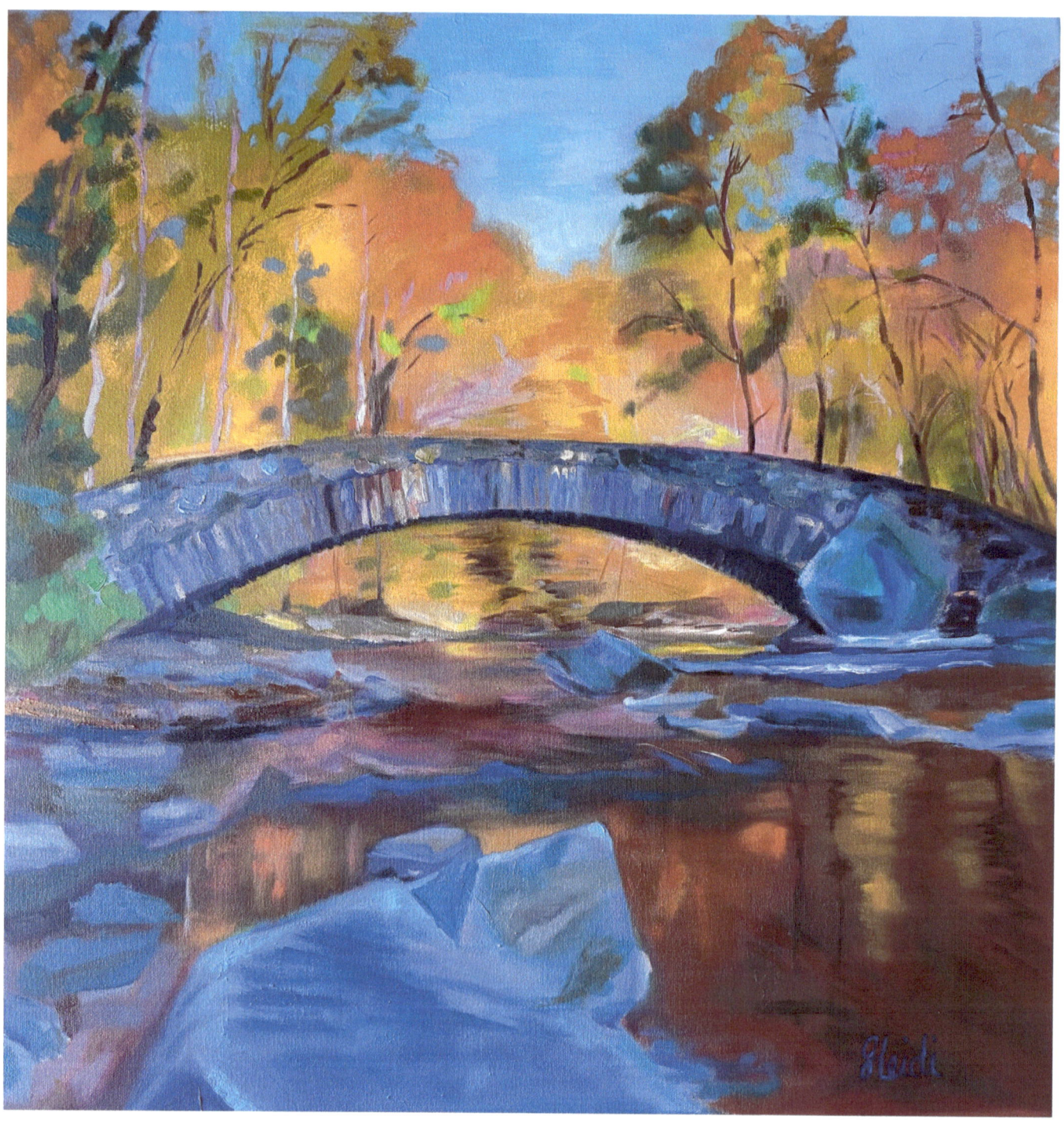

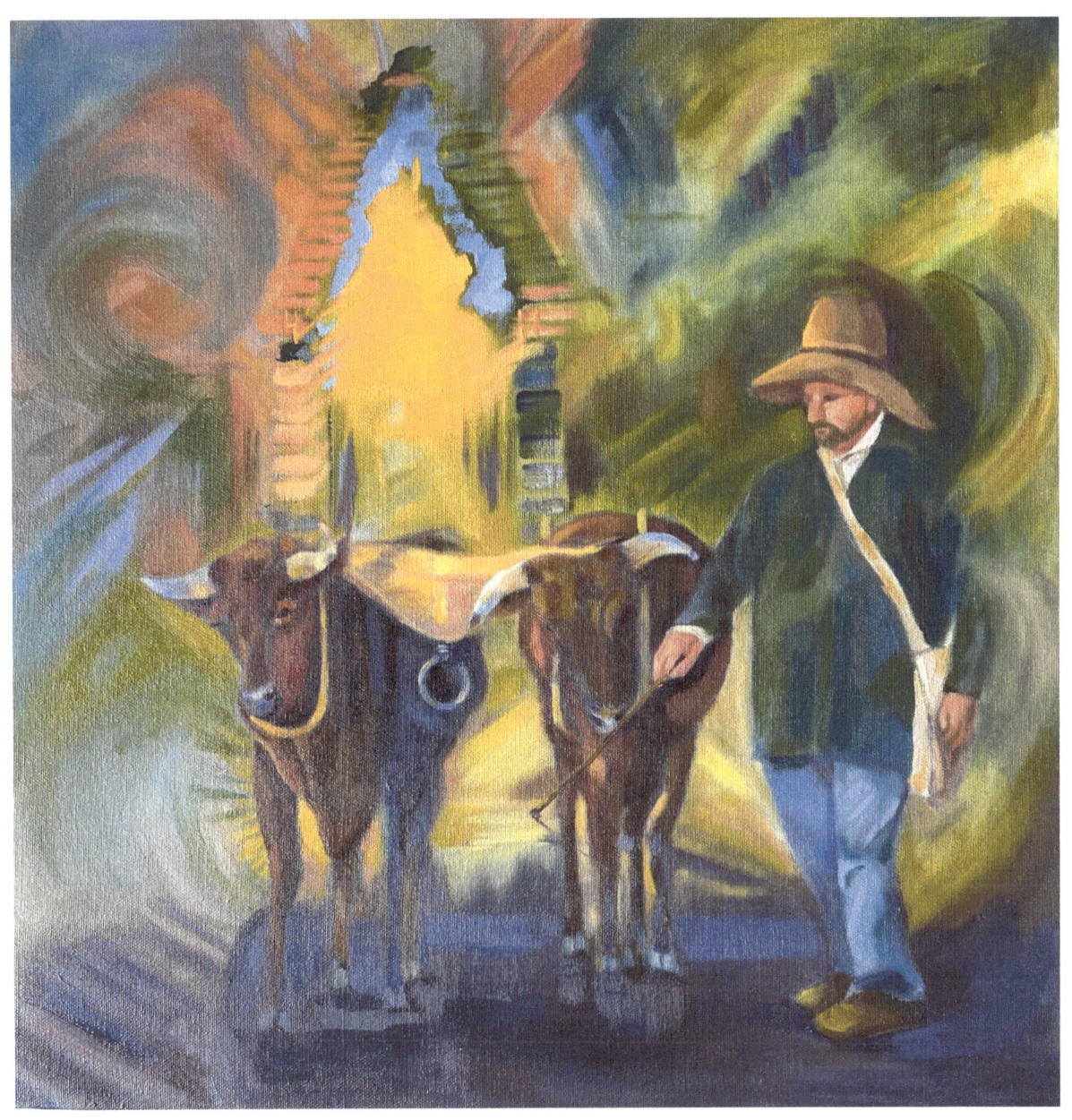

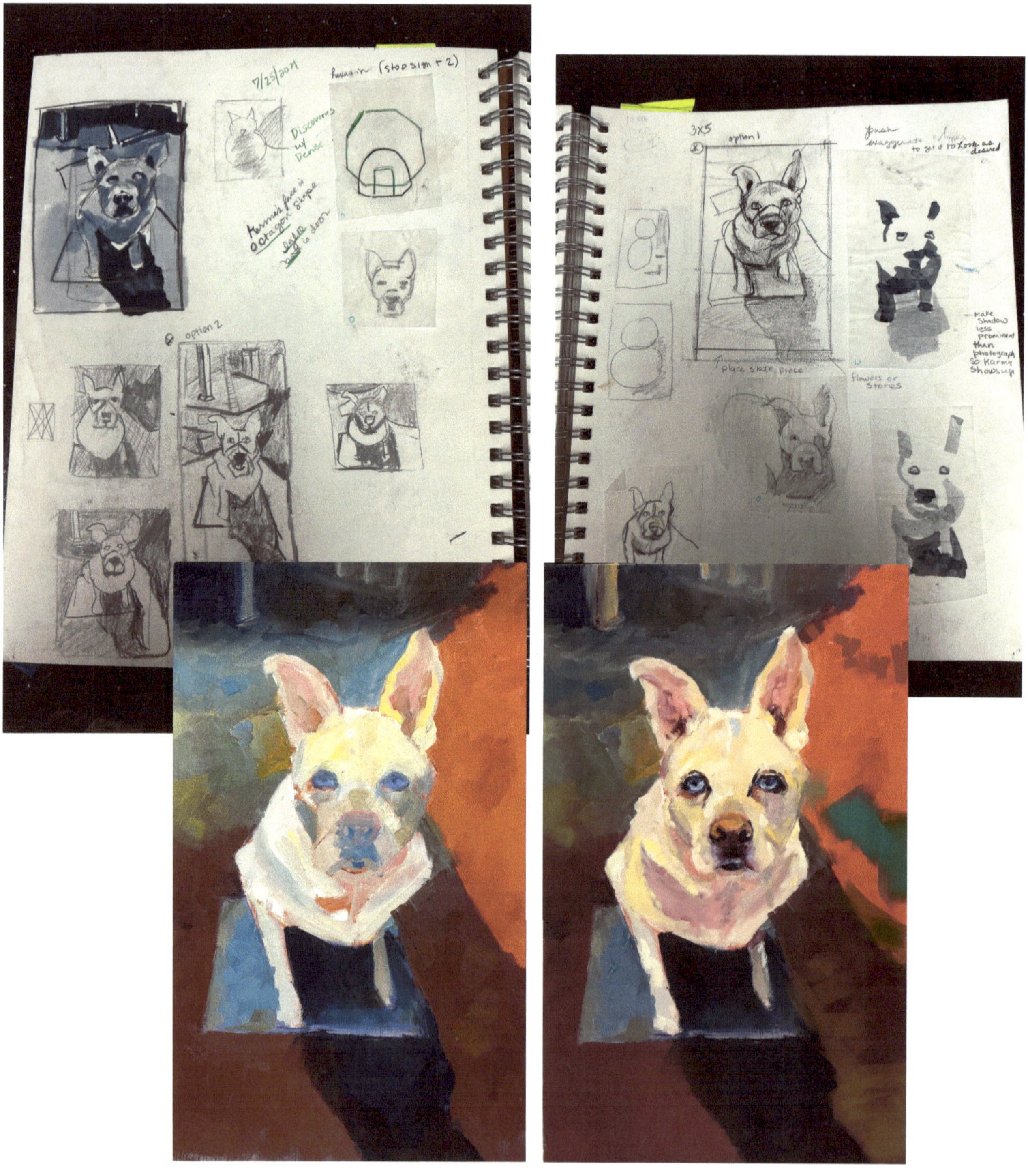

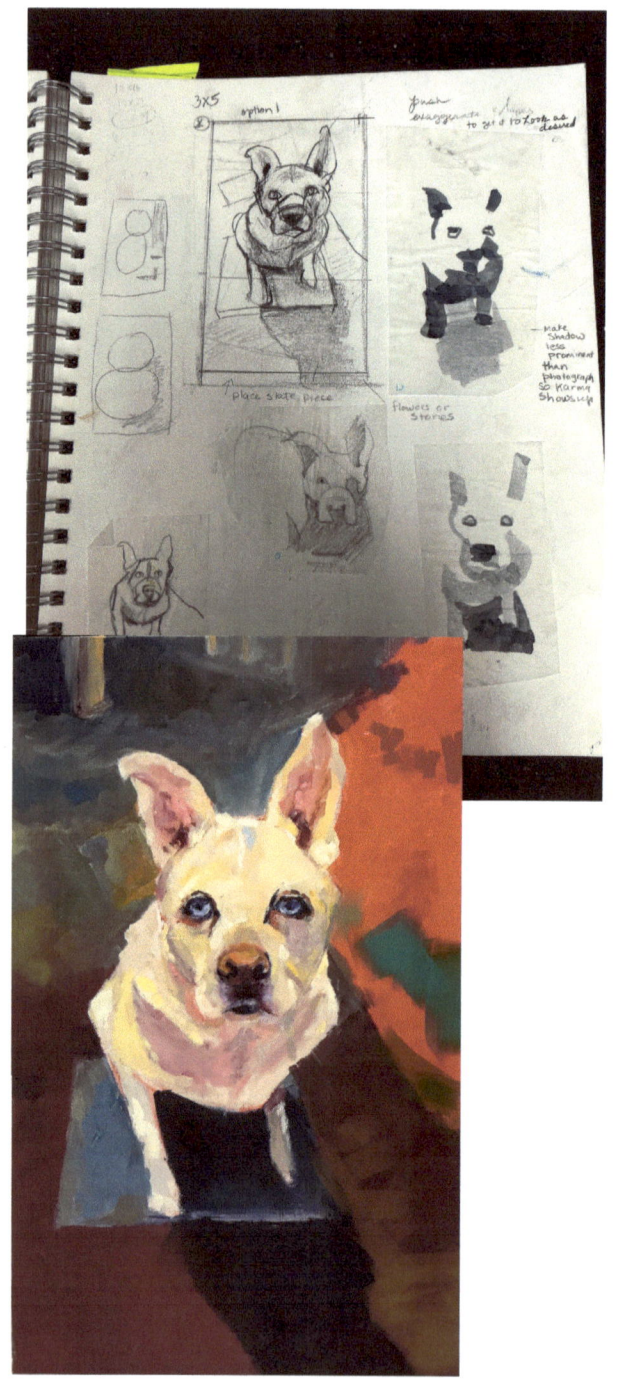

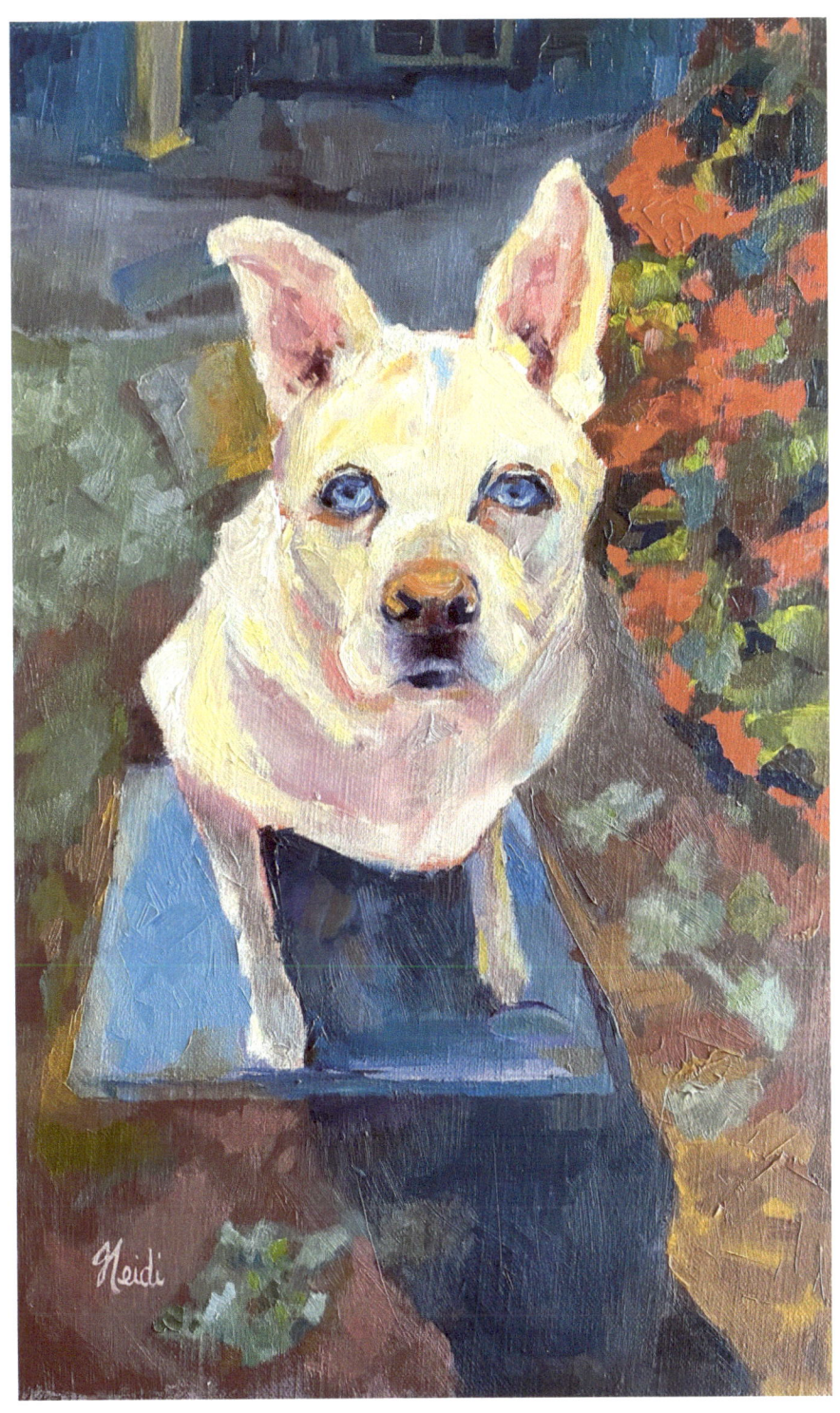

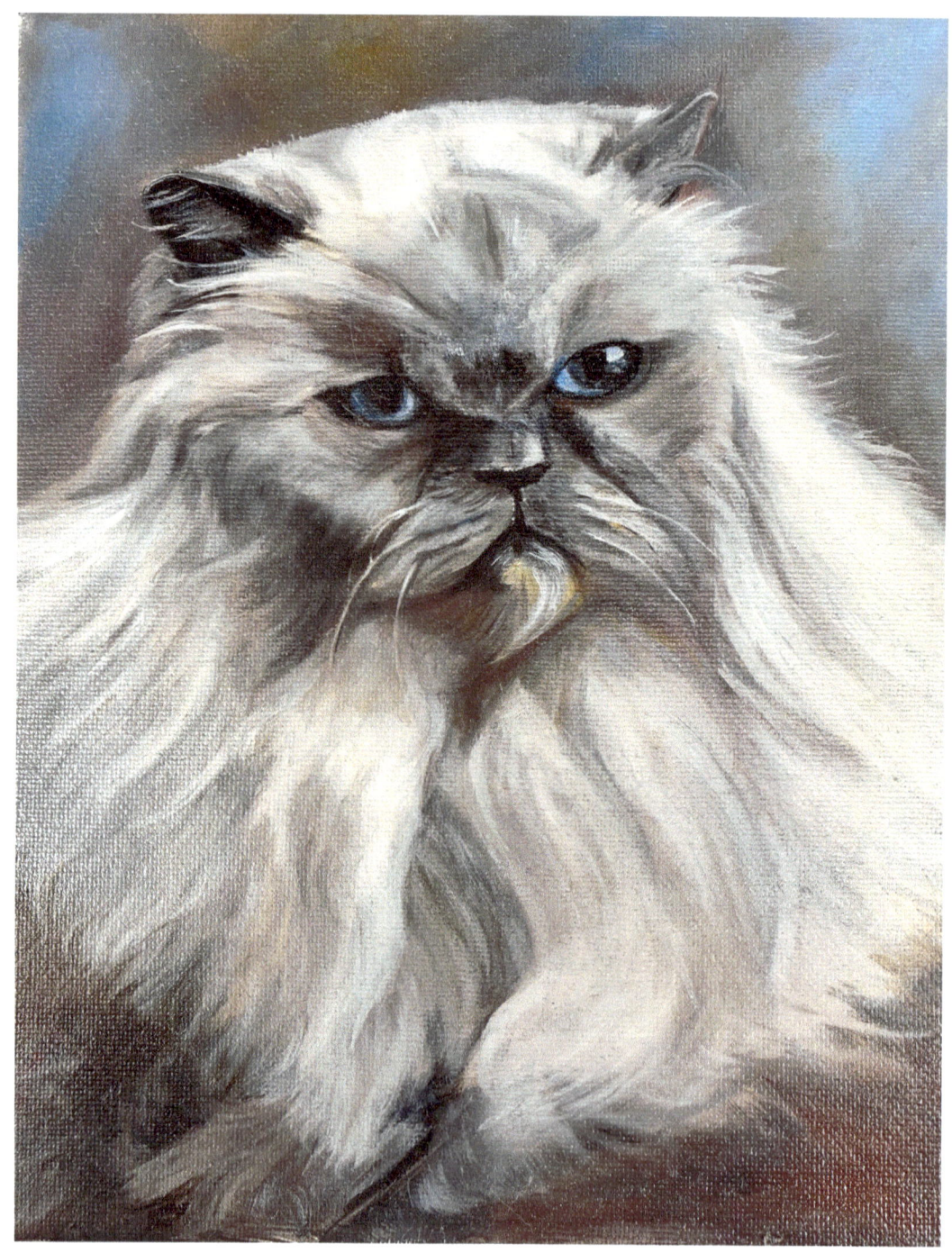

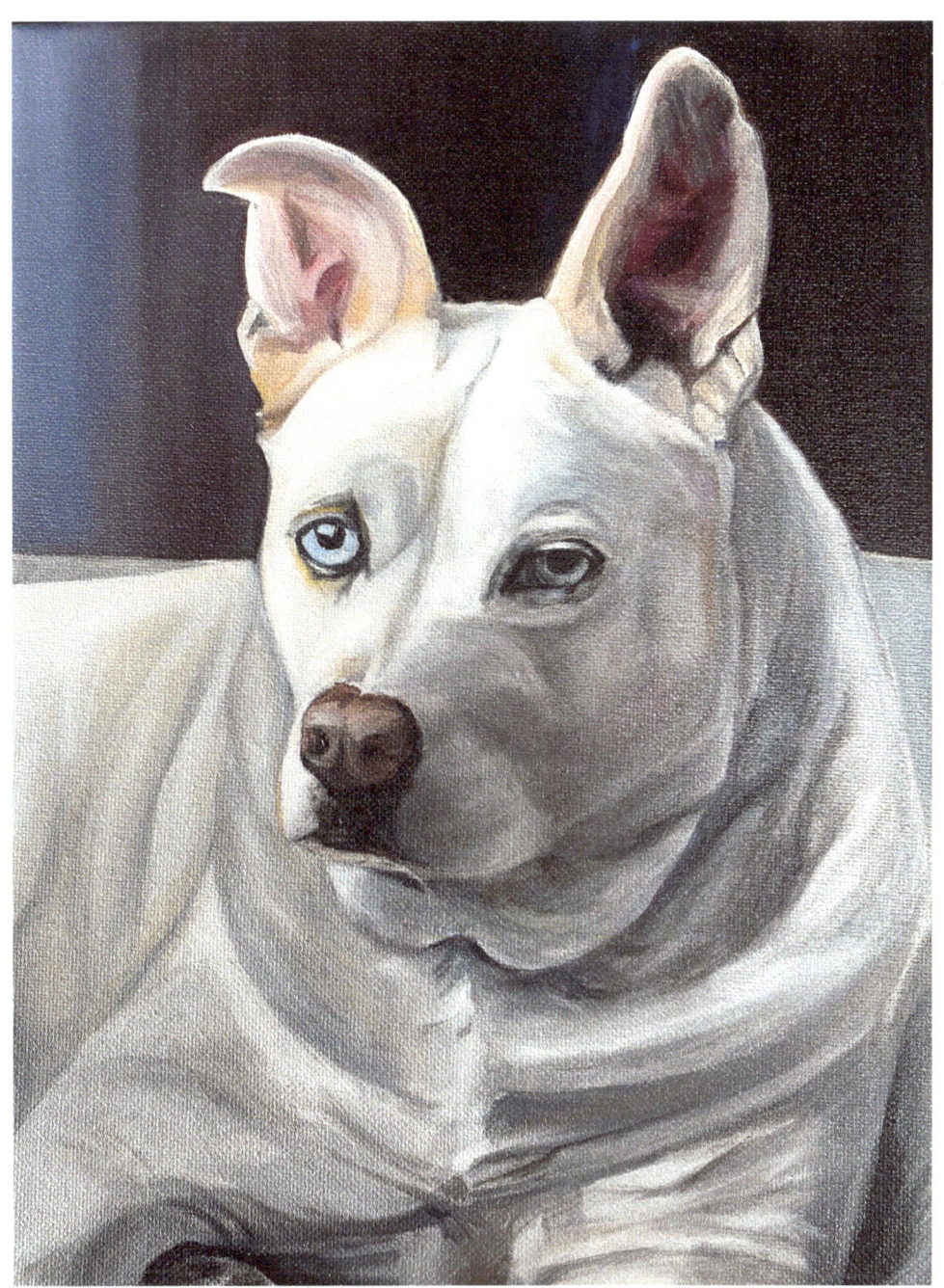

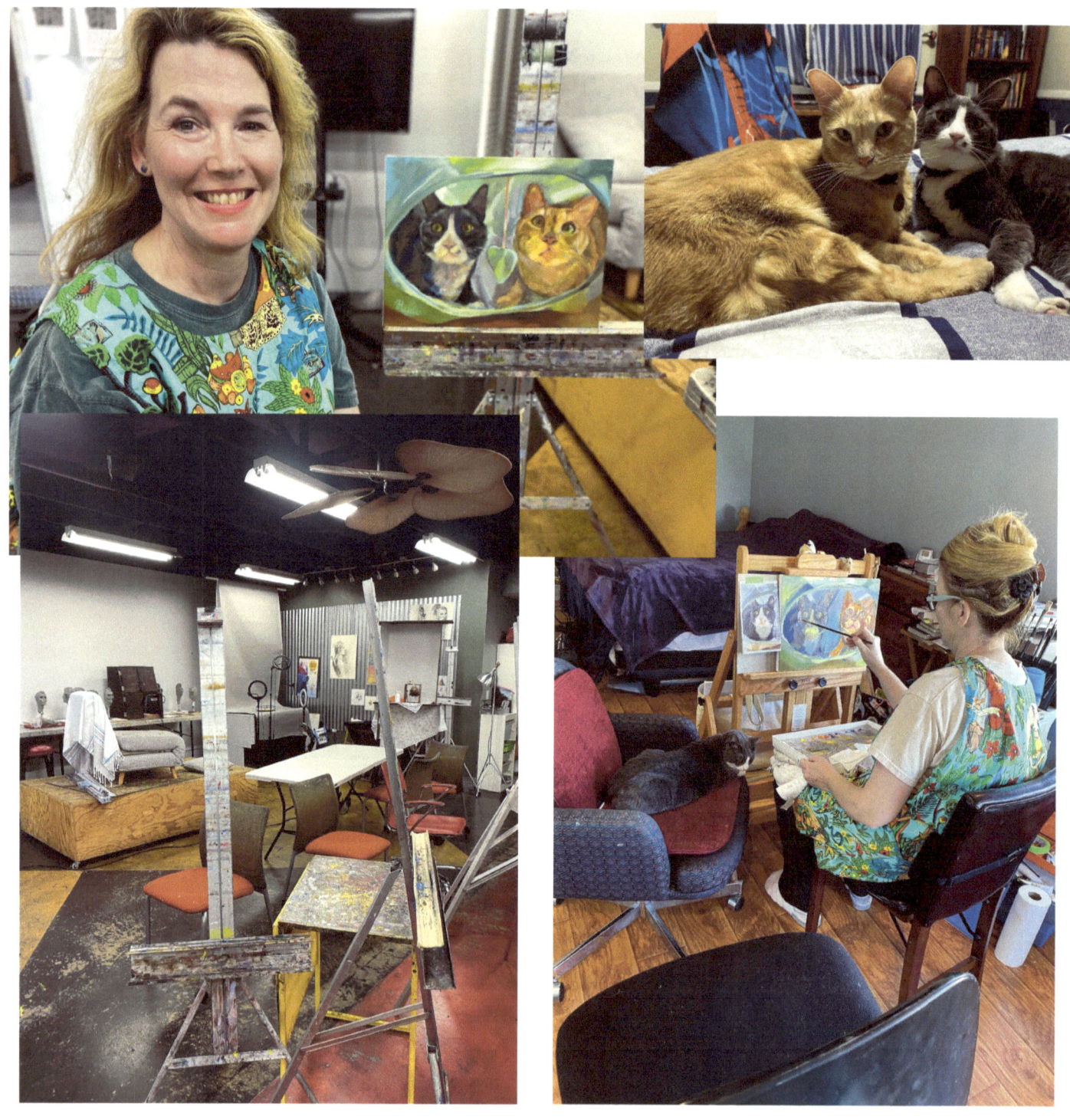

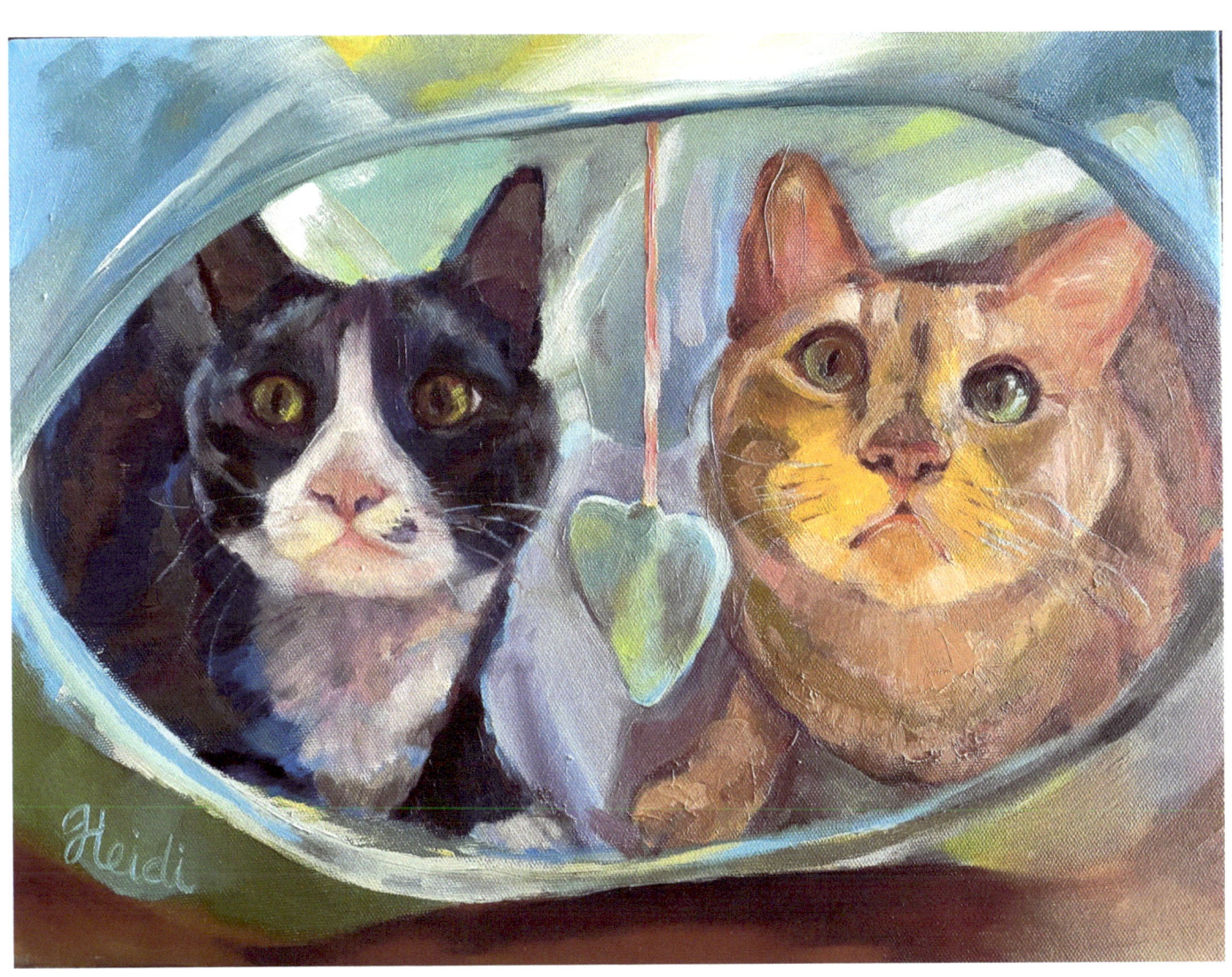

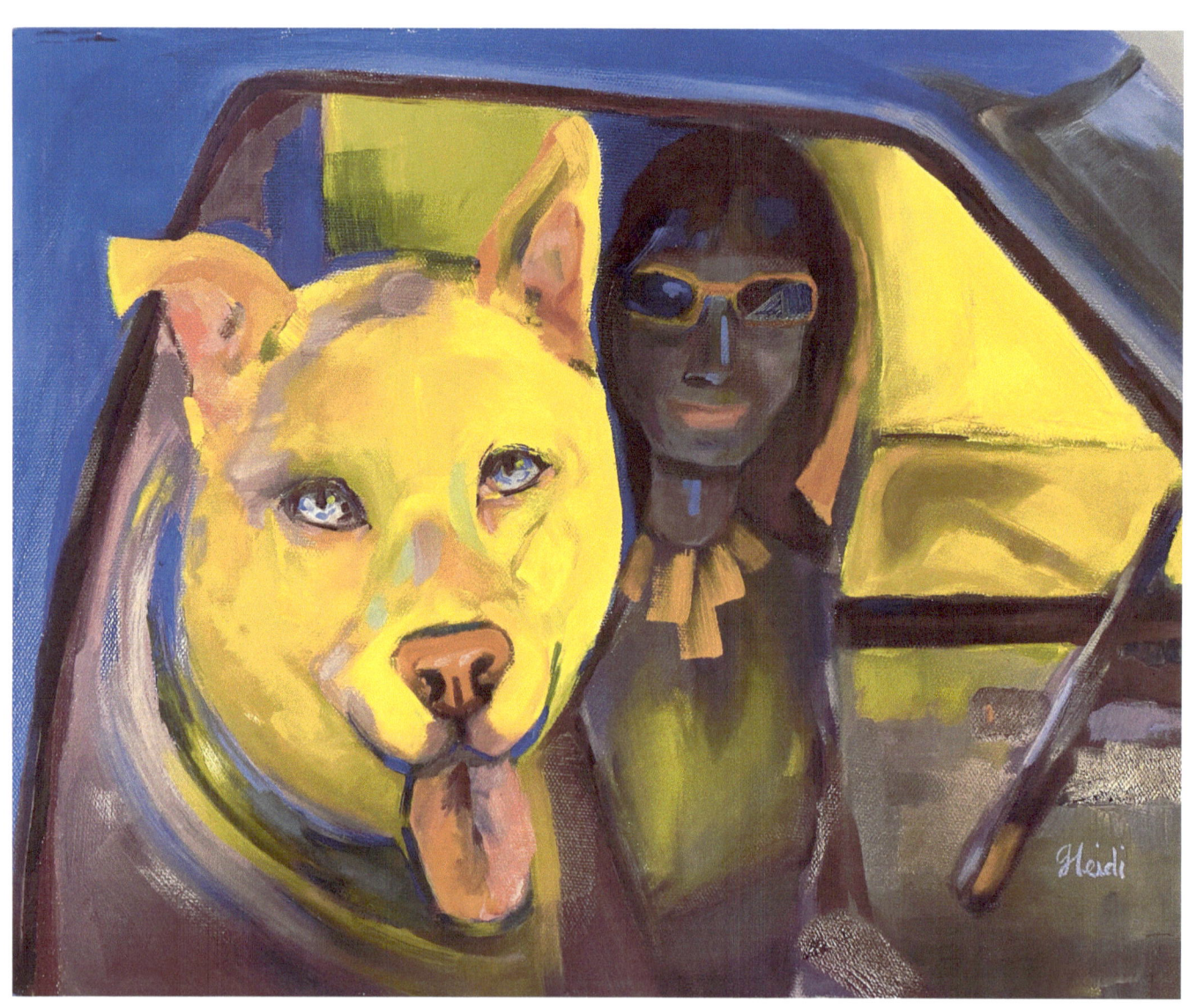

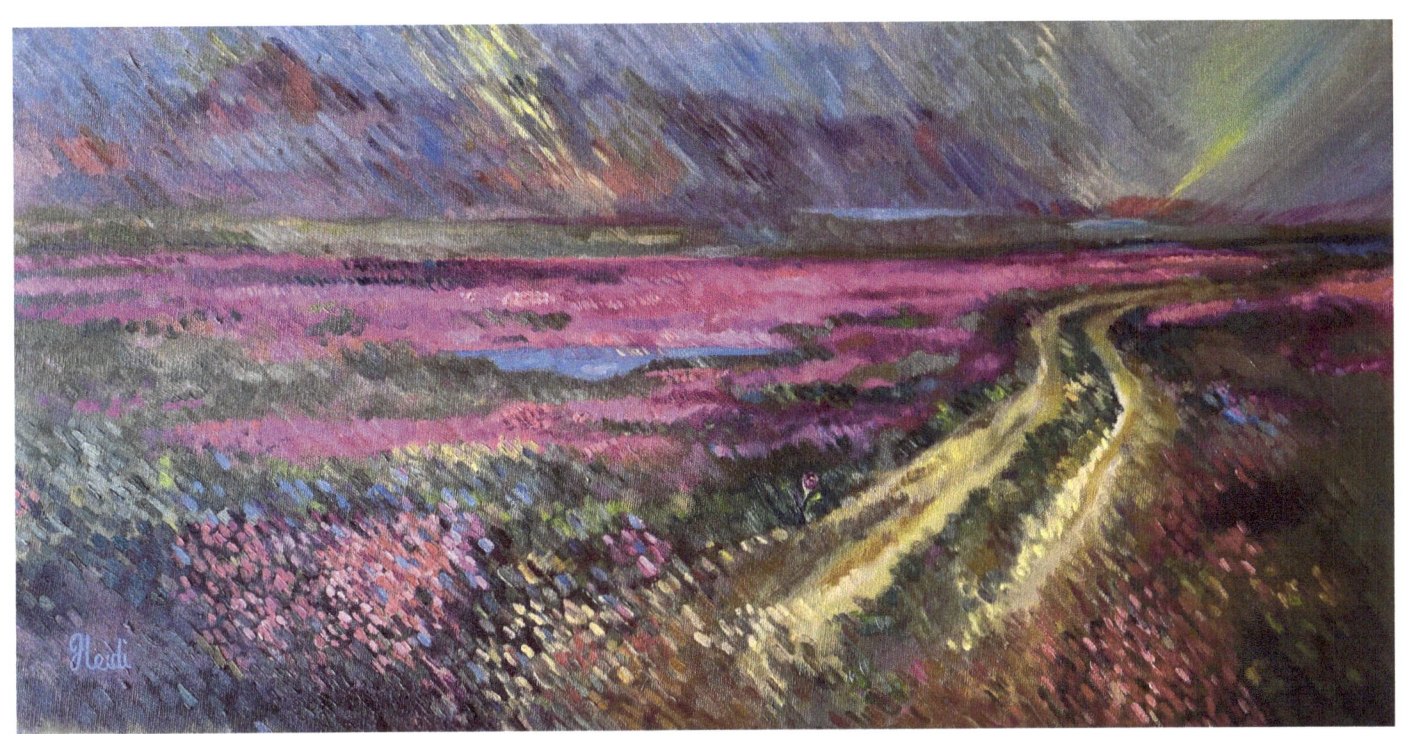

Jesus

THANK YOU:
Thank you to my family and friends at The Art Studio who have been so encouraging and supportive of me throughout the years.